# Generational Resilience

## Breaking Generational Cycles

Diana Oskov

Revealed Mind LLC

Diana Oskov



This book was written without the use of artificial intelligence tools.

ISBN - Hardcover: 979-8-9956841-0-7
ISBN - Paperback: 979-8-9956841-1-4
Library of Congress Control Number: 2026911670

The author of this book does not dispense medical advice or prescribe the use of any technique as a form of treatment for physical, emotional, or medical problems without the advice of a physician, whether directly or indirectly. The intent of the author is only to offer information of a general nature to help you in your quest for emotional, physical, or spiritual well-being. In the event you use any of the information in this book for yourself, the author and the publisher assume no responsibility for your actions.

Cover design by MKDesignLife

Editor Natalie Karneef

For more information, or to book an event, contact:

diana@revealedmind.com
https://www.generationalresilience.com

First Edition: June 2026

# Dedication

**To my loving husband, Nasko,**

I dedicate this book to you for all those times you stood by me. You have been my constant support and unwavering strength through the highs and lows of life. You have always been there to show me the truth, bring joy to my life, and make things right when they go wrong. Together, we have chased our dreams and made them come true.

You have been the one who saw me through it all, lifting me when I couldn't reach it and giving me the faith to believe in myself. You have been my voice when I couldn't speak and my eyes when I couldn't see. You saw the best in me and made me a better person.

Because you love me, I am everything I am today. You gave me wings to fly and touched my hand, allowing me to touch the sky. When I lost my faith, you were there to give it back to me, reminding me that no star was out of reach.

You have stood by me through thick and thin, and because of your love, I have stood tall. With your love, I have had it all. I am grateful for each day that I get to spend with you.

I dedicate this book to you, my loving husband. Thank you for being my rock and always standing by my side.

**And to my two kids, Daniel and Annabell,**

For coming into my life and filling it with much love, laughter, and joy. For teaching me and allowing me to see through your eyes. For showing me the true meaning of unconditional love and being my constant source of inspiration and motivation. You both have brought so much light into my life and have taught me to appreciate the simple things in life. Watching you both grow and learn has been the greatest joy of my life.

I dedicate this book to you both with the hope that one day, you will read it and understand the depth of love and gratitude I have for you. May this book inspire you to chase your dreams and to always believe in yourselves. Remember that anything is possible if you work hard and never give up.
I love you both more than words can express, and I am forever grateful for the gift of being your parent. Thank you for being the reason behind everything I do and completing my life.

# Table of Contents

Generational Resilience

*"You are given this life, because you are strong enough to live it."*

*- Robin Sharma*

# Introduction

Babies don't come with an owner's manual. And yet, we have to learn, somehow, the power of our thoughts, beliefs, and emotions. That responsibility falls to our caregivers, society, and culture. Our parents and caregivers plant the first seeds: of trust, of safety, of love. Of protection, belonging, and proper care. At least, that's what they're expected to do.

Instead, more often than not, these people subconsciously shape how we show up in life. We inherit beliefs and thoughts from our parents, and, often, the emotions that go with them.

These emotions are connected to past experiences that were never processed and became locked in our bodies. Our feelings are one of the primary navigation systems for our behavior. If they are unprocessed, they begin limiting us sooner or later. Thoughts drive feelings and feelings drive thoughts—a loop of patterns that condition our body to operate from the past, rather than from the present. The body becomes the mind. Our thoughts can run us, and our feelings can own us.

That's what this book is about.

It's also about my journey in learning this lesson. I'm about to share one of my hardest moments with you, and the awakening that came with it. How I learned that the seeds that are planted when trust is broken–when safety is not present, and when love is conditional–grow into weeds. And then we dim our gifts with labels, beliefs, and other people's doubts. This is not about blaming others for who we are. It's about understanding that what happened to us in childhood was not our responsibility, but as adults, it is now our task to become aware of how it's still limiting us.

It's my deep desire that we all use this awareness to become generational cycle-breakers. That we all understand why we are where we are in life, and become empowered to weed our own garden, to plant new seeds, and to grow something beautiful.

As an RTT therapist, I've had the honor of helping people create meaningful change in their lives. My clients come from a range of socioeconomic, ethnic, and cultural backgrounds, but they all struggle with or are unaware of their feelings. They have low self-confidence, or low self-esteem, or both. They struggle with sleep, live with imposter syndrome, and battle perfectionism. They're recovering from abuse or long-term addiction or both. I'm so privileged that these people have trusted me.

I don't have all the answers. But I hope these pages will inspire you to start to find your own.

Carlos Castaneda said, "We either make ourselves miserable, or we make ourselves strong. The amount of work is the same." Henry Ford said, "Whether you think you can or you think you can't, you are right." Does that mean that anyone can do or achieve anything they imagine as long as they believe hard enough? No, it does not. Consistent action, creativity, and commitment all play a role. But one thing is certain: if you don't believe something is possible for you, it's not. Period, end of story. The moment you tell your brain, "That's impossible," or "I can't," or "That will never work with me," you are 100% right. You'll command your brain to shut down, and your mind and body will follow. Our brains tend to reinforce what we already believe. All our beliefs are choices, and choices can be changed. Any limiting belief can be erased, replaced, or upgraded. While our potential as individuals is unknowable, what we know for sure is that limiting beliefs guarantee limited outcomes.

Belief is where it all begins. When you change your beliefs, you change everything. Our beliefs either propel us toward or prevent us from living up to our fullest potential. Our beliefs determine whether we fail or succeed, and how we define success in the first place. Beliefs are the genesis of every remarkable discovery, every leap forward humans have ever made, from science to sports to business, to technology, and the arts. The power our beliefs have over our lives cannot be overstated, but before we begin to change them, it helps to understand where they come from.

This is why I want to tell you my story in detail. I want you to see how all the beliefs I had shaped me, and how changing some of them had altered the course of my life.

The fact that you've picked up this book tells me that we have something in common: we are both students, and we are both seekers. I don't know the details of your history and hardship, but I do know that your inner power is immense. Your potential is limitless. You are unique, valuable, capable, and worthy of the dreams in your heart. Most of all, you have what it takes to transform and transcend whatever challenges you face and become the architect of your life. All it takes is one new perspective or tool. Remember, our minds are what give us the power to manufacture reality, both for ourselves and others.

The most powerful words in the universe are the words you say to yourself. The most powerful opinion in the world for yourself is your own opinion. Only you can take control of your garden and clean up the weeds. You are the only one holding the power to change you; to create positive and significant change for yourself and your future generations.

Happy reading!

# Generational Resilience

*"Who looks outside -
dreams;*

*who looks inside -
awakes."*

*- Carl Jung*

# CHAPTER 1

# Lifted

In the winter, my family disappears into the mountains.

The spectacle of the peaks of snow… the silence… the power of nature: this is our happy place. On the slopes, we reconnect with ourselves. We are silly. We are free. We become a unit in the mountains. And although no one pushes anyone beyond what feels right for them, we all love speed and how it processes the adrenaline our bodies store throughout the week.

But in the winter of 2020, something else happened in those mountains. Something I could never have predicted.

My father had been sick for five years. His organs were slowly failing. His liver was functioning at 20%. He was in and out of the hospital and needed frequent blood transfusions.

The doctors had already saved his life a few times, and

I had convinced myself they would continue to do so—partly because all of this was happening on the other side of the world. I left my hometown of Plovdiv, Bulgaria, in 2003 to immigrate to the United States. My parents and twin younger brothers still lived in Plovdiv, where, for the last five years, without complaint, my brothers had been helping my 60-year-old mom take care of my father. They responded to emergency calls. They sped him to the hospital. They had found friends to donate blood so he'd have another chance to live. They kept me updated by phone and video, and I visited regularly, but it still felt like I was "watching the movie" from afar, while trying not to give unnecessary advice.

My husband, Nasko, and I, along with our twelve-year-old son, Daniel, and our ten-year-old daughter, Bella, lived in Seattle. We normally ski an hour and a half outside the city at Stevens Pass, but this particular February, clueless about how drastically the world was about to change with COVID-19, we'd taken a trip to Vail, Colorado. One night in our warm rental apartment, after watching the groomers work the slopes, we went to bed early, dreaming of the fresh corduroy we'd hit tomorrow.

Shortly after midnight, my phone rang. It was my brother, Hristo. My heart pounding, I pushed the green button to accept the call.

"Sis," Hristo said, quietly. "Dad passed away half an hour ago."

The world went silent.

"The funeral home will take him shortly," my brother continued, his voice off in distance. "Everything needs to happen quickly. There are too many uncertainties related to COVID, and we want to avoid complications. I have to go. I'll call you back as soon as I can."

He hung up.

I stared at the black screen.

This couldn't be happening.

There would be no more miracles.

No more Dad.

And so much pain in the place where he used to be.

My stomach plummeted, and a flood of memories rushed in. The first time my parents had visited the States, for our wedding. Nasko and I, flying to Bulgaria with Daniel when he was one year old. My parents visiting us after Bella's birth. My father building a sand castle with Daniel; hiking with tiny Bella in a backpack. I had thought I was prepared for this moment, but tears started to pour. Nasko held me as my questions erupted between sobs.

"How is he just... gone? How can there be life without him? Did we do everything we could to help him?"

Nasko reassured me that we had, but of course, I still had questions. My dad was only 61 years old. I lay awake most of the night, all my thoughts fighting for space, coming around again and again like racecars never reaching a finish line.

Why him? Why now? Why couldn't they have saved him again?

In the morning, when the kids woke up, I tried to force a smile. They entered the room, and took in the silence.

"Is it about Grandpa Mutsy?" Bella asked, using her favourite nickname for their grandfather.

I opened my mouth, but no sound came out. Very faintly, I shook my head yes. They rushed to envelop me in a hug, everyone crying, which in a way was the best medicine I could have asked for. We sat together, and I sobbed until I had no tears left (until the next day. It's incredible how our sadness can replenish itself overnight).

Amidst this ocean of grief, I knew I had to make a decision. Should I get the first flight to Bulgaria? A lot had come to light about the Coronavirus in the five days we'd been in Vail, but there was still so much we didn't know. Would I be able to come back? My husband and kids were my lifeboat. I didn't want to be away from them. I sat, frozen, wishing someone would decide for me.

We called my brothers. Of course, they had no answers to my questions and were dealing with a lot of logistics.

"It's your decision," everyone kept saying. "We'll support you no matter what. There's no pressure to come."

But it didn't feel that way. It felt like no matter what choice I made, I'd carry the fallout forever.

I heard my dad's voice in my head: "Dida, focus on what is in front of you. Those who are gone are gone; you can't bring them back. Enjoy the kids. They are the future."

Was it really him convincing myself not to go, or was it me?

In the end, I decided to stay with my family. My mom and brothers supported me completely. I still had some guilt, but the decision felt right. Or so I thought.

With the COVID situation evolving, my brothers arranged the funeral for the next day. On my side of the world, my grief felt like a tiny, dark room with no windows and walls, closing in on me. But around me, the famous, sweeping back side of Vail Mountain—the legendary Back Bowls—sat at 11,250 feet. The view is soul-expanding; almost spiritual. It felt like fresh, life-saving oxygen.

In the end, we decided to stay in Vail for another three days, and ski.

It felt like giving my grief permission to fly. At the top of those snow-laden peaks, I was weightless, soaring through the cloudless blue sky before being pulled back down into the heavy, aching confines of my body.

When we returned to Seattle, Nasko took some family days off from work. The world had not yet shut down, so we sent the kids to school in the mornings and went hiking together in the afternoons. In the evenings, we'd sit together at the dinner table and share memories of my dad with the kids. We'd share them by phone with my mom and brothers, too. I bounced through the stages of grief completely out of order, from "this is not fair" to "just give me a bit more time with him"; from "this can't be happening" to "I will never be happy again".

Walking felt impossible, but Nasko, Daniel, and Bella were my crutches. They never asked how I was feeling. They just hugged me or sat with me when I needed silence. It felt like we were healing together, which made the pain a tiny bit easier to bear.

In Bulgaria, we have a tradition that when someone in your family passes away, you bring food to your neighbors. I put my own twist on this, making my father's favourite foods: rotisserie chickens, salads and chocolate cake. I added a special dessert for remembrance, made of crumbled wheat with vanilla, cinnamon, tea biscuits, cocoa, lemon peel, walnuts, and powdered sugar. And I delivered all of this to two of the families who lived next door to us, who accepted it with surprise and then gratitude (especially the desserts). When COVID restrictions got tighter and we were discouraged from sharing food, I stood determinedly in line outside shops for four hours to buy the same meals pre-made and packaged, then carefully dropped them off on our neighbours' doorsteps.

On the weekends, since both Bella and Daniel were in race training, we would head to Stevens Pass to ski. One of those weekends, a month or so after my dad died, we were doing just that. The kids had race practice, so it was just Nasko and I together. We took the lift up, as we'd done hundreds of times before, and climbed off. I skied ahead of Nasko, then suddenly stopped in my tracks and looked around at the evergreens, the snow, the sky.

That's when it happened.

Something just… lifted away.

A shadow? A spirit? It happened in a split second. I gasped as if I'd had the wind knocked out of me. It was so visceral, so outside of what I understood, that I couldn't name it… but somehow, I knew what it was: a deep heaviness that I'd been carrying my entire life.

I loved my father deeply and fiercely.

I always thought I'd had a happy childhood.

But that day on the mountain, for the first time in my life, I felt free.

*"Adolescents need freedom to choose,*

*but not so much that they cannot, in fact, make a choice."*

*- Erik Erikson*

# CHAPTER 2

# Communism

I can remember the collapse of communism in flashes.

Watching the Berlin Wall fall on our black and white TV that was no bigger than a toaster.

The first legal demonstrations since the 1940s, when our leader, Todor Zhivkov, was removed from power and replaced by Petar Mladenov.

The hunger strikes. The university buildings being occupied. Thousands gathering in the capital city, Sofia, to call for the release of political prisoners; for free elections; for the end of one-party rule and.

I wish I remembered more details. But I recall, so clearly, what happened inside our local shop.

The walk to the shop still comes to me automatically: the tiled path that led directly there from our home. I can hear the hum of daily life. The neighbors chatting, birds tweeting. I can smell the scents of fresh bread and smoked meat drifting from the open door, inviting me in.

In the first nine years of my life, every corner of that store was always bustling with life. Butchers in white aprons moved swiftly behind the counter of the long glass cases stretched along one wall, which gleamed under the fluorescent lights, overflowing with meticulously arranged rows of beef, pork chops, and ribs. Their expert hands prepared any cut you could dream of.

Bread was delivered fresh every morning, the loaves crackling with warmth when you broke it open. The dairy section was packed with rows of fresh, local yogurt in glass jars with aluminum foil lids, teasing you with their creamy texture and slightly tart taste. Everything was laid out carefully and predictably but proudly, arranged to display the bounty of the land: a reflection of the well-oiled machine that was life in communist Bulgaria, all of it in its place, with no room for deviation.

Our education was also as assured as the changing of the seasons. Like all kids, my brothers and I went to public school. High school (grades eight to twelve) would be aimed towards a trade or a specific profession, and after grade twelve, you either got a job or continued on to higher education. Many people went to university, although you didn't necessarily study what you chose. Rather, you applied yourself towards what would make you fit best into the system. Most of the people in admired professions like doctors, architects, lawyers, and teachers had once been students who were ready to serve the party, but had not necessarily wanted to learn these subjects and no skills to practice them.

By the time you graduated, either from high school or university, a job would be waiting, chosen for you, as sure as the sun would rise each morning. People with strong connections within the party even knew where their desk would be. No one spoke of layoffs or unemployment. I cannot recall anyone being poor, but neither can I remember anyone being wealthy, aside from the ruling party.

Even vacations were part of this system. Bulgarians spent two weeks at the Black Sea and ten days in the mountains every summer. Each company had its own resort, so workers would just take their families and go. I loved these times, jumping in the waves with my brothers while my mom and grandma hovered and my dad took photos of us all, or sleeping in a wooden bungalow with my grandmother's sister in the mountains, waking up to pick wild strawberries and make homemade jam. When I look at the pictures from our holidays back then, I can still smell the evergreen and sap in the mountain air.

For the rest of the year, like everybody else, my parents worked from 9 to 5, then came home and spent time with us. We had dinner together. They asked about our day and shared about theirs. They never judged us; they never reacted. Life felt happy, rhythmic, and safe. There was no feeling of stress, no pressure to be somewhere else or someone else, or to fulfill someone's expectations.

Not above the surface, at least.

**_"If I ever tell you about my past, it's never because I want you to feel sorry for me, but so you can understand why I am who I am."_**

_- Unknown_

# CHAPTER 3

# Chernobyl

It is not an exaggeration to say that under communism, the ruling party controlled everything.

If you wanted a car, even if you had the money to buy it, the party told you when you'd get it and what kind of car you could have. If you got permission to leave the country, which was rare even if you were representing Bulgaria at an international event, your passports would be held by an official who accompanied you, and your kids would have to stay behind in Bulgaria so that you would be sure to return.

Careers were also passed down through the family. In my case, my grandmother was a teacher, and my mom was a teacher, so I, in turn, was expected to become a teacher. Rarely did anyone jump ship and become something outside their family lineage.

The party owned people in ways you might have trouble imagining, even now. They took people's land; people's livestock. The mayor in my great-grandparents' village wanted to take away all of my great-grandfather's farm animals. My great-grandfather stood up to him, and shortly afterwards, disappeared. He did not return for over nine months, well after the party had collected all his farm animals and farmland.

A rumor spread that he had been sent to one of the labor camps, where they kept people without food and water for extended periods of time and killed them if they did not obey orders. My mom, who was a child at the time, asked him many times where he had gone. He refused to talk about it.

"I don't know what they did to him," she told me, "but he came back much more obedient. More fragile."

This is how you control a population.

When the Chernobyl power plant exploded on April 30, 1986, radiation levels in Bulgaria jumped by hundreds, even thousands of times. We were in the mountains during those days, and when my parents and their friends caught wind of the news, they believed so blindly in the government, they dismissed it.

"A couple of days later," my mom recalls, "we went to the market, and the lettuce was three times its usual size."

All the vegetables would be enormous that year, but the public was kept in an almost complete information blackout. We were given food in which radioactivity had been detected, while the party/"nomenklatura" (government officials and elites) drank only mineral water, washed themselves from underground water sources, and only ate meat and drank milk from cattle that drank safe water.

By May 24th, even though the radiation danger had not passed, the party officially declared it had. They lifted all restrictions, even the minimal ones introduced on May 7. But because some people were able to access BBC News* and had started to understand what was going on, the Bulgarian media had to start telling the truth. A year later, there was a second radiation peak. Foods in the grocery store chain, especially milk and meat and their derivatives, reached levels of radiation contamination close to and sometimes higher than the contamination levels of May 1986. Despite the warnings of scientists, the Bulgarian government refused to buy clean animal feed from abroad. In the winter of 1986/1987, they released radioactive food, harvested in May 1986, to feed farm animals. Radiologist Professor V. Bosevski called it the "Bulgarian Chernobyl", because this kind of denial went far beyond what was happening in other communist countries.

***

Four years after Chernobyl, communism came crumbling down.

At our once-bustling local shop, a small table was set up at the front door, where a cashier sold the sorry selection of the scraps they had left. The glass in the deli cases now reflected barren shelves and cold steel. Milk and yogurt came in small, sporadic deliveries, if at all. And bread–something so simple, so basic–became a luxury, rationed out carefully, each loaf like gold. To buy it, you had to present a coupon.

The emptiness of the store mirrored the shift in the people in our community. Instead of the chatter and laughter of days gone by, there was silence and drawn, sad faces. Where there had once been an easy assurance of full shelves and full bellies, now there was only tension and fear. We were hungry. Would there be food tomorrow? Would we make it through another week? Would we soon starve? The air hung heavy with a despair no one had the words for. Each day seemed to stretch longer as people braced themselves for whatever blow might come next.

Neighbors who had always smiled at each other and exchanged warm greetings now walked with their heads bowed. Waiting for the elevator one day, I saw a woman who lived in our building. She had always been vivacious and light-hearted.

"Good day!" I chirped.

"As good as it can be," she replied.

For most people, collective fear had taken over, and it was front and center of all their thoughts.

But some... this new, unknown world made them want to spread their wings and fly.

# Generational Resilience

*"Many will choose stabil-
ity of slavery
over
uncertainty of freedom"*

*- Marcus Aurelius*

# CHAPTER 4

# The Collapse

Most Bulgarians of my generation have a few, if any, photographs from their childhoods. I have hundreds–and home videos, too.

The party chose where you lived and how big your home would be, but you still had to pay rent, of course. Because my parents had three kids, the party allotted us a 900 Sq ft, two-bedroom apartment. We all slept happily in one bedroom, with a room divider between us toddlers and my parents. And my father turned the other bedroom into a darkroom.

I can still see him dipping the paper and developing the pictures, using special photo paper and his two tubs of chemicals. He would hang them on a clothesline with clothespins, a fascinating process to my three- or four-year-old brain. Even before my brothers were born, he'd even bought an 8mm film camera and had begun making silent family movies.

He tried to give us everything his parents hadn't given him. He heard somewhere that it was good for children to care for fish, so he built us four giant aquariums. Each one had a sand floor, and he even installed special lighting to provide the perfect temperature for the fish.

"Caring for the fish will teach you to care for others as well," he said.

My dad had never fit into communist life. He had the kind of mind that was always searching for new ways to do things—rules couldn't contain him. One of our neighbors offered to help us emigrate to Canada after communism fell, and my parents did consider it. But (as they told me later) it felt too uncertain with three young kids. And I know now that they were thirsty for freedom and innovation.  My dad held such hope for a better future, and wanted to contribute to it in any way he could.

In 1990, it was leaked that the government election results had been falsified. The broadcast of information was suspended as part of a blackout, but people began to rally. University students went on strike, blocking transportation at the entries of the major cities. When my parents came home from work that night, my dad was bursting with excitement.

"There are barricades going up at all the entrances of the city! There are people who have been there all day long! We have to go support them!"

My parents lined us up in the kitchen and we all made sandwiches with everything we had in the fridge. We filled thermoses with tea, brought all of this to the barricades, and distributed it to the protestors. And we joined them. As 10- and 8-year-old kids, we saw those barricades that blocked the entrance to the city as our playground.

Shortly before the collapse, my dad had rented a yard in one of the closest villages to Plovdiv, where he built a massive tent greenhouse. My parents had ordered 2000 mushroom blocks of twenty inches cubed each, and two tonnes of special ash to put on top of them.

Good thing they had three kids, because it was a *lot* of physical labour. They turned it into a game, and we happily helped move the bags in the greenhouse tent, and put the ash on top. We all shared the excitement when the first mushrooms started to appear, those tiny white dots rising out of the black powder, so surprisingly crisp and white. We helped pick, clean, and sell them in front of one of the big supermarkets. It didn't feel like work to me. It was more of a quiet satisfaction of being able to contribute, of being a team, where everyone did their part.

Because of the gas shortage at the time, we kids had already been transferred to the local village school.

My dad told us, "We have one tank of gas. We will save it for a real emergency. For everything else, we will have to use our legs."

So we carried the mushrooms six kilometers away to sell them in front of a supermarket. To motivate us to walk that much, Dad would buy us aşure, a Turkish dessert of boiled cracked wheat made with dried fruits and nuts. I loved it to the point that I couldn't wait to do the twelve kilometer walk so I could have it again. It's still one of my favorite desserts.

As we sold the mushrooms, my dad would talk to people and make new friends. Bulgaria had manufactured all kinds of merchandise during the communist regime, but most was exported, or if it was sold locally, it was in very limited quantities. When communism fell, the export contracts fell with it, but factories were still producing. My parents saw this as an opportunity to be entrepreneurs for the first time. One man we met was selling a kind of woven shoes that had only been exported before.

"Petar," my dad told the man. "I see you're selling out every day. I would like to do this for my family, too. I promise I won't interfere with your business. I'll find another location."

"Nasko," Petar said, "you are my friend. I see how hard you work with those three kids, and how involved every member of your family is. There is enough business for everyone."

This is one of the less-talked-about aspects of the communist mindset: how people understood that working together means learning more and prospering more, not less. "If I got here, I can bring you along and show you how I struggled, and we'll both be stronger for it", as opposed to "I won't tell you my 'secrets' and let you struggle for yourself." Petar told my dad where to go, who to call, and how to get started selling the shoes. That evening, my parents strategized.

"The city officials are starting to charge people for permits to sell in the streets," my mom said. "It will be expensive."

"But that's in Plovdiv," my dad countered. "Will it be the same in smaller cities?"

He called one of his relatives in Gabrovo*, where he is from. They had never heard of such a thing. Since there was still a gas shortage, my dad decided to load as much as he could onto the bus to Gabrovo and sell there. Meanwhile, we would keep the mushrooms going back home.

And just like that, he became a traveling shoe salesman.

As the mushroom production began to wind down, my mom joined him on the road. We kids stayed home with my grandma. My parents' business started to expand, and they began selling wares from other merchants they had met, like Pepa, a woman who sewed and embroidered dress shirts. Dad found television sets from the biggest TV manufacturer in Bulgaria. Soon, they opened a store.

My parents, born to fly, took off as soon as they could. So many others raised in the system didn't realize they even had wings. Conditioned by so many limitations, they just kept going the way they had before. Even now, I still see people who are not aware of what is possible for them. They don't realize they can do something totally different from what they've been taught to believe.

# Generational Resilience

*"Love felt by the parent does not automatically translate in to love experienced by the child"*

*- Dr. Gabor Maté*

# CHAPTER 5

# Strong Girl

Business was booming for my parents. Soon, they had a big shop selling things no one had seen before in Bulgaria: clothes, color TVs, VHS players, cosmetics–all made in the country, but never before available to Bulgarian people. And the Bulgarian people were buying. My parents traveled more, and found more new merchandise. The business kept growing.

Money was visibly present, although I didn't understand it then. I can't remember ever needing anything. My brothers had Nike sneakers, which were rare. In fact, we all had nice clothes, although I never cared about brand names.

When we took holidays, we stayed in the biggest suites at the best hotels, but my parents were always working. They'd leave us with our grandmother, spending maybe a half day or a day with us to show us the significant historical sights of wherever we were. It was as if they might miss something if they took any time off.

At home, my brothers and I made a schedule so we'd know when to clean the house and wash the dishes. We went to school with a key around our necks, and when we got home, we played outside until one of the mothers yelled for her kids to come back. (The unspoken rule was that when one mom yelled, everyone had to go home.) My parents rarely had time anymore for the family dinners that had been a cornerstone of my existence since I was born, so my brothers and I began to make our own: printcesa (bread covered ground meat and spices and maybe cheese, baked in a small toaster oven) or tsiganska banitsa (bread brushed with sunflower oil and sprinkled with savory spices). Most kids' parents would check their homework after dinner. (If it wasn't done correctly, you were supposed to start again from zero.) We checked our own homework, or sometimes, my grandma would look it over.

My grandma was around a lot during that time. She was only 40 when I was born, and my parents had pushed her to retire early. She had never remarried after her husband died and had dedicated her life to us. She held that traditional belief that you sacrifice yourself for your kids (and later, when they get old, they sacrifice everything for you). I don't believe in this "exchange", but I am also so grateful for my grandma's presence in our lives. It took many years for me to understand how important it was. She never criticized us or tried to control us. She always encouraged us, and taught us a lot of lessons about responsibility—like how if we want to have a clean house, we had to participate in cleaning it.

She tried to keep the family dynamic as steady as possible with my mom and dad working so hard, but still, we often went to bed before my parents returned. They came home very late, sometimes in the middle of the night. The next morning, they'd either be asleep as we left for school, or leave before we were even awake. Any time we spent with them felt precious, but they were very fixated on providing us with material things, like juice that came in boxes, or jeans that weren't available to most people. I think it was their way of making us feel like part of their world.

And unlike my grandma, they didn't praise us very much. We were raised to be strong. I, especially, was charged with taking care of my brothers.

"That's your job as the big sister!" they'd call out to me as we went out to play.

One day, a big group of us found a big sack of empty 1.5 liter plastic bottles. Someone came up with the brilliant idea that we'd chase each other with one of these bottles, and when you got close to your target, you'd tap them with your bottle, and they'd be out of the game. The whole block got caught up in the action until Rado, one of the boys in our neighbourhood, hit my brother, Ivo, on the head. Ivo started bleeding heavily.

"You cracked my brother's head open!" I screamed at Rado.

Then I punched him in the face.

It was an instinctive action, not one anyone had taught me to do. I felt instant relief, and then a twinge of guilt. Rado ran home with a nosebleed, and we went home, too. I was scared about what was going to happen to me, and to Ivo. After all, I hadn't fulfilled my parents' expectations as my brothers' caretaker.

My parents happened to be home that day. My dad opened the door to find me crying, and Ivo's head pouring blood.

"What happened?" he gasped.

I was bawling and in so much shame, I couldn't answer.

Ivo stepped in. "Dida broke Rado's nose to protect me."

"Yeah," Ico added, admiringly. "She did well."

My mom took Ivo to the bathroom to clean him up. Ico filled him in on the details. I was still visibly in distress, so my dad put his arm around my shoulder.

"Strong girls don't cry," he said.

I thought, "Am I strong? What made me strong?" I was afraid to ask out loud, but it made no sense to me. How else could I process what had happened, aside from cry? This was my body's natural reaction.

But in Bulgaria at that time, people did not "do" emotions. I know that might sound strange from the point of view of Western culture today. It wasn't that people struggled with their feelings; they just weren't aware of having them, which meant that expressing them didn't happen properly, either. Even my mother and grandmother, both of whom had been preschool teachers, did not talk about feelings. And we had never been given guidance on how to deal with situations with friends.

So there I was, my tears still pouring while I gasped for breath.

My dad looked at me, confused. "Why are you still crying?"

At that moment, the doorbell rang. It was Rado and his mom. She was furious that a girl had given her son a bloody nose. My dad stood like a giant stone in the doorway, waiting for Rado's mom to stop yelling. Ico and I hid behind the open door, listening.

"Do you know why my daughter hit your son?" Dad asked, when Rado's mom had finally calmed down.

"No, and it doesn't matter. She is a girl, and you should teach her some manners."

(For a girl to fight was a huge cultural no-no at the time, where girls and women "belonged in the kitchen". But my dad had always instructed us: "Never attack first, but if someone attacks you, protect yourself to the best of your ability.")

"My girl has plenty of manners," my dad said. "You might want to take better care of your son, who split my son's head open."

My mother appeared next to us at the door, holding a bloody towel.

Rado's mom went quiet. Then she turned to her son and started yelling at him.

The situation resolved itself eventually. Rado's mom apologized, my dad accepted, and Rado, despite his best wishes but with his mom glowering down at him, said sorry to Ivo. And just like that, as kids do, we were all friends again.

My parents never punished me for what I'd done. In fact, my father commended me for it, although he reminded me we don't need to hurt back as revenge.

But that day solidified several beliefs in me. First, that it's an older sibling's job to be responsible for the younger one(s). I always felt I had to take care of my brothers, even when they were old enough to take care of themselves and didn't need my help. I was constantly on alert for their safety and wellbeing. This was not empowering. It robbed me of my own experience of just being a kid.

And second, that I was not allowed to be weak. "Strong girls don't cry", they just keep going and doing, without connecting to any feelings. Feelings were meant to be stored in a deep, dark place—out of sight, out of mind.

Materially, at that time in my life, I had everything I needed and more—unlike many kids in Bulgaria. But the idea of parental presence or warmth—these simply didn't exist for me. I would still trade all the material comfort I had and more to not have been charged with the responsibilities that should have been theirs. To be allowed to feel everything I felt, which is our birthright as humans. And mainly for the chance to have spent more time with my mom and dad.

My father made close to 400 videotapes of us growing up. But for so much of our childhoods, he wasn't actually there.

And he never watched those videotapes again.

*"If we are not prepared to think for ourselves, and make the effort to learn how to do this well,*

*we will always be in danger of becoming slaves to the ideas and values of others due to our own ignorance."*

*- William Hughes*

# CHAPTER 6

# Mafia

During the post-collapse years, the Bulgarian mafia operated at every level. If you paid your dues, they "protected" your business (from them). If you didn't, your business would be gone the next day.

Much like the party once did, the mafia believed they owned everything.

In addition to the stores they were running, my parents had begun a yarn business. They built a small manufacturing facility with state-of-the-art machines of different sizes. They would eventually hire a team of employees, but until then, I'm sure you can guess who operated those machines... my brothers and I, even though we were still teenagers. Together, we created yarn from beginning to end—the entire production process, right up until the actual yarn ball. Like with the mushroom business, we felt proud and fulfilled to be part of what our family was creating.

The business was scouted by an Italian company at an international trade fair in Plovdiv, and soon, my parents were exporting directly to Italy. An Italian businessman even offered to buy the company, but my dad wouldn't sell, as he believed we would continue to grow. Resellers were lining up to buy my parents' yarn; meanwhile, they had started importing Wrangler and Levi's jeans—brands that were not yet available in Bulgaria—and selling them from the same warehouse where the yarn was manufactured and sold.

To celebrate his thriving business, my dad decided to buy a rare Soviet car: a GAZ-24 Volga. It was one of a handful in the country.

In no time, the mafia found out about the car.

The phone calls began.

The mafia knew when my father was home. The phone would ring either early in the morning or late at night. My parents never hid anything from us, so we knew what the calls were about.

"Just ignore it," my father would say.

But if he didn't answer, the phone would ring and ring.

He wanted to be stronger than them. He started to drive us home, and then he would drive the car to a secured garage, where a guard would watch it overnight. But the threatening phone calls continued. The mafia simply believed that the car should be theirs.

This was about much more than just the car, for my dad. He hated dishonesty and the idea of people taking things that did not belong to them. His belief in justice was stronger than his fear. My parents had worked so hard to buy this car. No one had handed them anything, so they weren't going to hand anything over to the mafia.

Unfortunately, this is a naive philosophy when it comes to dealing with organized crime.

The air in our house became tense. One day, my father came home with a gun. He wore it during the day, every day, instructing us to never touch it unless he was around. He became increasingly worried for our safety, especially that the mafia would kidnap us. He hired bodyguards to take us to school and back. If we were on the second school shift, the one from 1pm until 7pm, the bodyguards would come pick us up before school ended because they were worried about us being out after dark. We kids didn't understand enough about what was going on to be scared, but having someone walk us to school and back felt very strange.

My dad taught us to never give up. Find a way until you can't, and figure out your options from there. This legacy of his has gotten me through many difficult periods and helped me see many opportunities that might not have been obvious.

But he also taught us that if things got dangerous, it was time to change plans.

With the car, his love for his family won out. Our safety was more important, no matter his principles or how much he enjoyed having it.

So he sold it to the mafia.
He painted it a different color first, just to make a point.

# Generational Resilience

*"Whiners find ways to
complain
while
winners find ways to suc-
ceed"*

*- Joe Polish*

# CHAPTER 7

# Banks Collapsed

The car incident taught my parents that if a Bulgarian person showed how much money they had, the mafia would decide it was theirs. So, financially speaking, they began to lay low. We never knew until much later how much they were actually earning at that time. (We still don't really know, but it must have been a pretty comfortable amount.)

Then, one morning in the spring of 1996, so early that the world still felt blurry and my body hadn't yet caught up with my mind, I was brushing my teeth when I heard an unfamiliar, uncomfortable chatter in the kitchen. The cadence of my parents' conversations was almost always calm and rhythmic, like a song. This felt very different. I could sense the fear. Then, there was dead silence.

Any icy dread crawled up my chest.

I walked into the kitchen. My parents were both standing deadly still, staring at each other. The morning light cast sharp lines across their expressions–the shock in their eyes, the tense set of their jaws. My mom was holding it to the counter as it was going to collapse. My father, usually so composed, looked confused.

The silence was unbearable.

"What happened?" I whispered.

At first, it was as if they hadn't heard me. And then, slowly, my mother turned to me, her lips trembling. "The banks collapsed overnight. We have no money. We've lost everything."

I stared at them. This couldn't be right. How could something so essential, like banks, just collapse? Where did the money go? I wanted to ask, but my voice didn't work. It was like I'd been punched in the stomach. Everything felt dark. I had never seen my parents like this before.

Between 1996 to 1997, Bulgaria faced one of its most severe financial crises. Widespread corruption and self-dealing between banks and their political sponsors led to inflation rates skyrocketing to over 2000%. People watched helplessly as their hard-earned money became practically worthless overnight, while prices soared. Shelves in stores emptied once again. Those who could afford to stocked up on essentials, leaving others to scramble. This further eroded faith in the government's ability to manage the economy, fueling helplessness and frustration.

About one third of banks halted their operations or went bankrupt at that time. State-owned and private banks collapsed. This exacerbated the turmoil, and the Bulgarian Lev plummeted in value against foreign currencies. Imports became prohibitively expensive, isolating our country even further as we struggled to stabilize internally.

Protests erupted as the Bulgarian people demanded accountability and change, their voices amplifying the call for government reform. The government did take steps to stabilize the economy and restore public confidence. A more aligned government formed, with radical economic reforms.

And I remember the feeling like it was yesterday.

One moment we had plans, stability, the promise of tomorrow. The next, nothing. This loss—sudden, jarring, like a cold wind that takes your breath away—left me with beliefs about money that burrowed into my mind for many years. For me, the banks collapsing compounded a story that was born when communism ended: that money was a mirage. One day it's there, solid, tangible, making the world go round, and the next, it's gone. It slips away when you think you have a hold on it.

In the spin of the days that followed, my dad collected himself and said, "You are only left with the people around you. Sometimes, that is all you need. We are healthy and alive. We will recover and make more money again."

This sounded warm and comforting in that dark time.

But as I worked on this chapter, I asked my mom about what she remembered, and she shared a much harsher reality.

"Your father came dangerously close to having a heart attack," she told me. "More than once."

Looking back now, I can see the exhaustion and the fear behind his smile. I can hear the way his voice sometimes wavered when he talked about "tomorrow." I wonder what it must've been like for him, after his years of ceaseless working–from the mushroom business and our one and only tank of gas, to losing it all, and standing on the edge of collapse, holding the weight of our world in his hands, trying to keep us from seeing how fragile it all was.

He thought he never let us see how close he was to breaking under pressure. But it was during this time that I started to notice his drinking. I call it quiet drinking, because he was never abusive to us, he just sat in front of the TV, descending into numbness, there but not there. The next morning, it would be like nothing had happened. And the next night, he'd do it all over again.

He became moodier and more agitated. He started to get annoyed at small surprises, like a friend showing up unexpectedly at the door. We began walking on eggshells, always making sure to tell him in advance of what was going on. My mom would buzz around him like a bee, trying to calm the situation. We never talked about it. We just knew whether Dad was in "a mood". And this hypervigilance and fear of conflict–mine or others–stayed with me for many years to come.

We all got swept up in a storm we didn't know we were in. My dad had grown up with so much trauma, not that I knew anything about that yet, and he desperately wanted to keep things as structured and predictable as possible, because that seemed to be the only way to feel safe. He was so addicted to freedom that he built his entire identity around providing. I didn't understand how close we were to losing something far more significant than just money.

Nothing is black and white. My parents were fiercely determined to bounce back from their losses; to survive whatever life threw at them. They taught me how to stand up after a fall, wipe off the dust, and keep moving forward, even when the road ahead felt uncertain. But they did not teach me that we need to pause and reflect after we've been knocked down.

We need to take the time to learn from the suffering in our lives. It is this kind of understanding that breaks us free from repeating the same patterns we, and our parents, have done many times before. If we don't learn–if we don't stop and take the time to destroy those generational cycles–we become slaves to them ourselves.

*"Every time I thought I was being rejected from something good,*

*I was actually being re-directed to something better."*

*- Dr. Steve Maraboli*

# CHAPTER 8

# Herbalife

After the banks collapsed, I watched the exhaustion etch itself more deeply into my parents' faces as they grappled with the remnants of their dreams and the weight of surviving.

It was especially evident in my mother. Her once sparkling eyes went dull. Her vibrancy seemed to fade under the weight of her burdens—weight she gained physically, too, as she reached for food for comfort and energy. I started to long for the days when her laughter echoed through our home.

And that's when we stumbled upon the Multi-Level Marketing (MLM[1]) product, Herbalife[2].

I need to pause and say that I am not a fan of MLM.

---

[1] See Notes – p.295
[2] See Notes – p.295

It's an unfair system, with less than 1%[3] of participants actually making any money, and it often targets marginalized and vulnerable populations.

Nor do I agree with the body image ideals that have been placed on women. We should never judge anyone on how big or small they are, and if someone is physically unhealthy because of how much they eat, it is the mind that needs to be healed first.

But these were different times, and we were different people. Herbalife was something new and exciting to our ex-communist country, and everyone was searching for ways to get healthy, and ways to make money. The products promised to feed the body on a cellular level: to make you feel great, lose weight, and improve your skin.

I came across the brand by chance, and in it, I saw an opportunity to get my mom's fire back. She was searching for a way out, too, and was ready to try anything. The change was remarkable, and it was not just in her appearance. It was as if her inner light flickered back on. Within a month, the kitchen, which had become a place of quiet despair, once again echoed with her laughter and chatter as she prepared healthy meals with newfound enthusiasm. I felt like I had my mother back.

Everyone started asking her, "How?"

And she would tell, and then she would sell.

––––––––––––––––––––

[3] See Notes – p.295

Seeing the business opportunity, my parents immediately jumped on board. They sold almost all the yarn and clothing stock we had left–the jeans, the machines, everything–and our lives changed almost overnight. They were back on the road within months, traveling across Bulgaria, reconnecting with old friends, and introducing new ones to Herbalife. They shared their story and offered others an opportunity to build a better future.

Their energy and determination were infectious. I was only seventeen and still in school, but I, too, became immersed in the business. While my parents were away, I dove headfirst into the excitement of entrepreneurship, building my own sales team in Plovdiv, teaching them what I had learned. I devoured self-help books like there was no tomorrow–"How to Win Friends and Influence People" and "How to Stop Worrying and Start Living" by Dale Carnegie; "Winning People Over: 14 Days to Power and Confidence" by Burton Kaplan; "The Seasons of Life" by Jim Rohn. No one told me to read these books, and they weren't available in bookstores or the library–communism would never allow it. My interest in human behaviour had been ignited.

Soon, despite the economic struggles everyone was facing, even more people found a way to join the Herbalife movement. People in our community were desperate for a way to make money, find stability, and improve their lives. They were hungry for opportunities, and we were offering them a lifeline

Weekends became a whirlwind of energy. People traveled to Sofia from all over Bulgaria to the workshops, which were all-day affairs filled with motivational lectures, dynamic speakers, and music that set the mood. They networked, laughed, and bonded over shared dreams of success. It felt like we were all part of something bigger than ourselves. It felt like a movement that could change lives.

And amid all that newfound excitement, there was Nasko.

This boy with the same name as my father was the DJ at many of the Herbalife events. With his dark brown hair, thick eyebrows, and infectious smile, he caught my attention as I watched him keep the energy of the room high and had us dancing well into the night. He seemed focused, attentive, calm, and thoughtful. And so approachable.

At first, I watched him from a distance. I saw how he would play upbeat music during training sessions to make sure no one fell asleep. He could read people, effortlessly guiding the crowd onto their feet for cocktail hour and beyond, knowing what would make them move and have a good time. We would dance all night. No one wore high heels the next day.

I continued to attend the events as the months rolled on, soaking in everything I could and silently hoping for a chance to connect with Nasko. The first time we spoke, I learned that his parents were also part of the Herbalife community. This common bond gave me courage, and my spark kept growing.

More months passed, and I patiently waited for something to happen. One day, I confided my feelings to my grandma. Her answer surprised me.

"Sometimes," she said, "if you want something that much, you should reach out and see if you can have it instead of one day regretting that you didn't try."

I had no idea how I was going to make this happen, but I was determined. Then, St. Atanas Day, Nasko's (and my father's) name day arrived. After a full day of training, some 1200 people gathered for a Herbalife party. My grandma's advice rang in my ears, along with my parents' teaching of always finding a way.

It was now or never.

I went to the front of the room and asked Nasko for the microphone.

"With the next song," I said, my voice echoing, "I would like to say happy name day to the two Naskos who are special in my life: my dad, and Nasko, our DJ."

The venue fell dead silent. I felt so alone, reaching out to this one person who had been on my mind for such a long time.

Then Nasko smiled. He put on a slow song and invited me to dance.

People were staring at us, but I couldn't have been

more proud of myself. We started dating soon afterwards. Our connection felt so easy. There were no expectations and never any pressure. We met each other's friends, watched movies, went for walks together, and reveled in each other's company.

One day, about six months into our relationship, Nasko and I met at a coffee shop. As soon as he arrived, something felt different. His movements were tense. He sat down across from me, and took a deep breath.

"My mom won a green card," he said. "We are moving to the USA."

My body went numb.

"This is it," I thought. "The end."

We sat in silence for an uncomfortably long time.

Finally, I asked, "What does this mean for us? Is that it? Are we done?"

He replied quickly, like had been rehearsing for my question. "I love you. I will be back for you."

But I couldn't hear him. It felt like I was drowning. It was like watching a movie of my life going on without me in it.

"No one ever comes back from America," I mumbled.

He hugged me. "I will be back."

And then he and his family packed four bags and moved across the world.

*"And ever has it been
known that love knows
not its own depth until the
hour of separation."*

*- Khalil Gibran*

# CHAPTER 9

# Away

It was the late 1990s, and during that time, in Bulgaria, people were stealing everything they could get their hands on. Mail would even get stolen out of mailboxes. Most of our building's mailboxes had been vandalized, and there was no law enforcement at that level. For this reason, my parents rented a mailbox at the post office.

So whenever a letter from Nasko arrived, the mailman would leave a note in the box in our building. I would check for those notes every day. Eventually, I learned that it took a month for a letter to get from Nasko in America to me in Bulgaria.

I still checked every day after that.

When the magical note would finally appear, I'd grab it and run to the post office to get Nasko's letter. I would open it quickly to make sure there was something in the envelope (this was the impact democracy had on us—there was so much lying and stealing from people and from every level of the government that even receiving an envelope made you question reality). Then I'd run back home, snuggle up in my bed and pore over the letter. I'd read it again and again until I remembered every word; every punctuation mark. I'd put it under my pillow at night and read it the next day, over and over, until the next letter arrived.

I missed Nasko so much. But I barely cried. Remember, sadness wasn't "allowed" in our world, and I was a "strong girl".

To avoid my feelings, I'd preoccupy myself with school. I did other people's homework because I was good at it, even though it enraged some of the teachers. My parents got us a computer, which was a big deal as not many people were able to afford one. The internet was in its early years, and we mostly had dial-up in Bulgaria, but it wasn't cheap. (Nor, at $2 a minute, were international phone calls.) So I'd still send Nasko letters by regular mail and wait forever for his letters back.

It was like in black and white movies, except we were teenagers.

Being apart from him felt like getting a rare toy and having it suddenly disappear. I knew he still existed, but I wasn't sure when I was going to get him back. What were we thinking? Why did we hang on, when it seemed so unlikely that we'd ever see each other again? It made no sense, but I could see how hard my parents worked for their relationship; how they rarely fought and how much they communicated about everything. I had watched my father cherish my mother throughout their marriage, and Nasko did the same with me. He refused to give up. So I believed it was possible, and my parents believed it for me.

"Just give it a shot and see what will happen," they told me. "Do what feels right for you. If it feels right, wait for him. If not, explore."

I know now it was a childish love in many ways. This is perhaps most obvious in many poems I wrote for him.

Why is there no comforting cigarette,

that I can smoke and forget the sorrow raging in my little heart?

Oh, I miss you, my darling,

and this sorrow no one can comfort even with a single night.

I want to keep this bitter sorrow and the dark day on which it came.

I want to forget this sorrow, but not you, the ruler of my heart.

Ah, how hard it is to live when you feel half whole.

For a girl who didn't know what feelings were, I sure had a lot of them.

***

I was so preoccupied waiting for the letters that time flew by. A year and a half passed, and Nasko returned for a visit.

It was Christmastime, and I was supposed to meet him at his relatives' house in Velingrad. My best friend, Emo, was going to drive me. (Tall and lanky, Emo had the kind of heart that shows up for you at 3AM without asking questions.) It was cold that December morning, and so early, most of the world was still asleep.

When Emo arrived, I looked at him and said, "I've changed my mind. I'm not going."

He laughed. "Are you crazy? We are going. It's my job to get you there and then drive you back here with Nasko."

"What if he's changed? It's been so long! What if we are both different people?"

"You have lots of questions. The only way to find out is to find out for yourself. We can't make Nasko wait for us. After all, he is coming from the other side of the world for you."

Somehow, Emo convinced me to get in the car. I begged him at least twenty times to turn around and drive back. He ignored me.

In what felt like no time but was actually an hour and a half later, we arrived in Velingrad.

I refused to get out of the car.

"Don't make me drag you in there and make a scene," Emo advised.

"I'm even more scared now. What if nothing is the same?"

"I am with you. If it is not the same, I promise we will leave right away."

We rang the bell and stood on the front porch. I couldn't breathe. I was sure my heart was going to explode. The terror was suffocating, but the love was overwhelming.

Nasko opened the door and held me tight for a long, long time.

It was as if he had never left.

Nothing had changed for either of us. Just time.

**"Strong women aren't simply born.**

**They are made by the storm they walk through."**

*-Unknown*

# CHAPTER 10

# Revoked

This tradition went on for several years. Nasko would come home every year at Christmas, and for one perfect, fleeting month, the world felt right again. Our bond didn't just survive the distance, it blazed to life the moment he walked through the door. Those weeks were magic for both of us, and I think everyone around us felt it too. My family, our friends—they'd light up watching us together, these two people who fit like they'd never been apart.

But after thirty days, maybe less, he'd be gone again. We packed a year's worth of love into those short weeks, knowing that goodbye was always waiting at the end.

Meanwhile, my parents spent horrifying amounts of money trying to help get me a visitor's visa so I could go to America to visit him.

I'd travel to the US embassy in Sofia, arriving before 8am. I'd bring every document that might prove I would return—bank statements from my parents, school notes, work notes... the more, the better (or so we believed). I'd go through security, wait in a courtyard until I was called, submit all of this (plus the very high fee), then go back to the courtyard and wait again until they called me for the interview. They'd look quickly at my paperwork, type something on their computer, ask a few questions (why did I want to go? How long had Nasko and I known each other? What reason did I have to return?)

And then, a black rubber stamp saying "REVOKED".

Every time.

It was one of the most expensive lessons of my life, not to mention my parents' lives. (My dad sold his professional video camera so they could help pay for all the application fees.) And each denial felt like a blow, not only to my plans but to my belief that persistence would one day pay off. But something in me kept pushing me forward, even though Nasko and I had no expectations or vision of how our relationship would evolve. Don't forget my family conditioning: fall, get up, brush yourself off, don't take time to reflect on why this might be happening, keep going.

I was constantly preoccupied by worry and fear, and also with hope: maybe this time would be it? In total, I applied for a visa to visit America twelve times. I got a new passport each time, which—although we didn't know it—was of no help at all, because I'd been flagged in their system, and they had a file containing all my paperwork and all of my rejections.

Every time, the reason for rejection was "Potential Immigrant". (Even back then, America had "too many immigrants".) I had no intention of actually *moving* to America—this was just to visit, although while it was going on, Nasko made me fill out a green card application every time he visited at Christmas. He'd take it with him and mail it when he returned to the States. This was because of a news story that had broken in Bulgaria when all the green card application letters were found in a big river.

Five years passed. The internet was still dial-up. The odds were still against us. No one believed our relationship was going to last. With every new visa rejection, even I was starting to lose faith.

By now, I was working as an interior designer and studying law and public administration. One spring day, one of our friends called and said he was going to come over and pick me up for a coffee. A short time later, the doorbell rang. I opened the door and saw a bouquet of roses as wide as our building's corridor. Nasko sent me flowers many times, but they always arrived in a big box.

My first thought was, "Why aren't those in a box?"

My second was, "Why are they moving?"

They moved a little more until Nasko appeared from behind them.

My legs melted out from under me and I leaned against the wall so I wouldn't fall. In the last five years, he had only ever come at Christmas. This year, he'd decided to spend his spring break with me.

A few days later, while Nasko was still in Bulgaria, a letter from America was delivered to my home. My dad thought it must be important, so he brought it over to my work. I knew instantly, from the sender's info, what it was.

My dad knew Nasko was at the travel agency that day, so he called and had the travel agent pass on instructions to Nasko to come to my work immediately. Nasko raced to my office, worried about what was going on.

I handed him the letter.

"You thought you were going to surprise me?" I said. "Look at that!"

He stared at the envelope. His eyes grew wide.

The letter wasn't a visa. It was a green card.

He lifted me up and twirled me around, as my dad stood outside, watching and smoking with extra intensity. Dad hadn't hugged me himself (remember, we didn't express our feelings), but I could see how he felt: the victory of having won after a long battle, and also the grief over what he was about to lose: me.

We celebrated at home that night, but with a lot of mixed feelings. Mom shared my dad's sense of victory, but I could see her struggle with the idea of me leaving. My brothers couldn't believe it. They were hurt and disappointed by all the rejections. I think they still are.

"Those Americans, they contradict themselves. They reject your visa but send you a green card?"

Everyone at work was thrilled.

"You're finally going!" they congratulated me.

"No I'm not," I told them. "I'm staying right here."

*"Not being able to speak is not the same as not having anything to say."*

*- Rosemary Crossley*

# CHAPTER 11

# No English

After all the trying and all the applying, the desire to go to the USA had been bled out of me. And I certainly didn't want to go and *stay*–I had only ever wanted to visit Nasko. I loved my life in Bulgaria. I finally had my parents back, living their full, joyful lives with our shared Herbalife success. I had friends. I had half a year left to earn my master's degree in law, and a great trajectory for work once I graduated. While everyone else (it felt like[4]) was trying to escape Bulgaria for a better future for themselves and their kids, I had no need for more. Plus, America wasn't a different country to me. It was a different dimension. It was somewhere I had only seen in the movies; a land from which most people did not return. Aside from Nasko's stories and from Hollywood, I couldn't predict or dream of what life could look like there.

---

[4] See Notes – P.295

But also, I could.

Because in America was the person who had taken my heart. That person who promised to come back for me, and did. The person who was "fighting" the days of separation with me. If I faced this unknown, I had a chance to build something with that person. When something costs you a lot, you value it more. What if going to America could be even better than the life I'd hoped for here?

Over the next ten months, my head was like a bouncy ball. Go. Stay. Yes. No. Was love strong enough to overcome the resentment and the disappointment that had built up in me from all those visa rejections? Could I actually make a life in a place whose language I knew only the words "hi" and "bye"?

My parents did believe that opportunities were available in Bulgaria, but they also believed in love. They wanted for me what they had for themselves. My dad couldn't stand the thought of me struggling to survive in this new world, so he encouraged me to take a nail technician class just in case I decided to move to America. I didn't have time to start learning English, but this was a skill I could learn quickly and take with me that wouldn't require much speaking. He wanted me to be able to open doors, even if I couldn't yet open my mouth in English.

"You're not going all the way to America to just wash dishes," he told me.

"Why not?" I said. "We don't have a dishwasher at home. I'm good at it!"

I actually loved beauty class. I've always been creative, and working with nails felt natural to me. The idea of bringing a skill to America gave me a sense of purpose, even though I still hadn't decided if I was going. I loved seeing people's delight at the finished product. Little did I know that being a nail technician meant more than just the work itself; that it involved connection and conversations, and is almost "therapy" for many clients.

As I filed and polished and learned nail art, and did the X-rays and health tests to be allowed into the States, I continued to swing back and forth about actually making the move. It never felt obvious to me. When I finally bought the plane ticket, my mom came with me, so she could make sure I wouldn't change my mind. And when it was time for me to fly, my dad called in a favor with his contacts at the airport so that he, my mom, my brothers, my grandmother and some friends were allowed onto one of the balconies so they could watch me board the plane, and be certain I was actually going.

> **"Only those who will risk
> going too far
>
> can possibly find out how
> far one can go."**
>
> *- T.S. Eliot*

# CHAPTER 12

# America

Never mind going to America... getting on an airplane for the first time in my life was already another world.

The cold seats seemed to suck me in. My home country already felt small compared to this giant plane, lifting me away from everything I'd ever known. The languages I heard sounded like they came from another galaxy. The flight attendants serving food and drinks... the clouds passing by my window... even the illuminated seatbelt sign... everything reminded me of how far I was about to go. There was already a hollowness in my chest for what I was leaving behind.

As we descended into Chicago, I gaped at the view of the grid of streets and endless stretch of highways; the rows upon rows of illuminated houses; downtown's gleaming high-rises, standing as silent sentries, welcoming newcomers like me. I felt tiny in the vastness of it all. Then, as we left the plane and entered the airport, I suddenly felt like I was in a scene from an American movie. Everything seemed bigger and louder. People were racing in all directions like they had done this many times before.

I trailed after my fellow passengers, desperately hoping they were leading me to the exit. Every emotion I'd ever felt was coursing through me, and it was impossible to feel them all, so I just focused on moving my legs forward, one in front of the other, pushing the cart with my luggage. Finally, I saw those sliding doors.

And there, on the other side, was Nasko.

He told me later he could see how terrified I looked. I know now that I was in shock. It was such a relief to see him, but it wasn't until we went outside, got into the car, drove on a twelve-lane highway (six times wider than any highway I'd ever seen in my life) past all the massive trucks along, and stopped at a gas station that I realized what I had actually done. I had just flown for fifteen hours surrounded by a new language I didn't understand, been ejected onto what felt like a new planet, and was actually here, now, with him.
I didn't know what I was going to do with any of this. But at least we were together.

87

*"We have to get use to the
idea –*

*at the most important
crossroads in our life
there are no signs."*

*- Eenest Hemingway*

# CHAPTER 13

# Crossroads

After a welcome dinner at Nasko's family's home, we headed out on another one of those busy highways to Urbana-Champaign, the town where he went to college. The unfamiliarity of the sights and sounds made my head spin even faster. And if that weren't enough, it was spring break, which meant that a few days later, I joined Nasko and three of his friends, all computer science majors, on a road trip to a biotech conference in Boston.

The friends welcomed me instantly, as if I had been a part of their group forever. But I was still a silent passenger in their world of English, never mind the tech jargon and inside jokes. They were so at ease in an environment that felt foreign to me. It was a glimpse into a life full of possibilities, far removed from my own.

We drove through endless highways, relying on paper maps, taking turns behind the wheel. Hours passed in a blur of highway landscapes, laughter and late-night gas station stops. The distances seemed insane to me. For the first time in my life, I felt the sheer vastness that lay beyond my hometown. The streets were so big and packed with people–all these millions of strangers with unknown stories. The sidewalks and subways pulsed with energy. The skyscrapers cast deep shadows and neon lights that never seemed to dim. Even the sky seemed bigger.

For me, every stop was a revelation. We reached New York, where I tried Moroccan food for the first time—couscous for dinner, which was a shock since we only eat it for breakfast in Bulgaria. I saw a flower shop that sold flowers from all seasons of the year, vibrant with colors I'd never seen all in one place. (In Bulgaria, we could only get flowers that were in season.) And then there was Subway. The idea of building your own sandwich was fascinating to me, though the flavors were an adjustment. Everything tasted unfamiliar. The biggest shock came when we managed an impossible reservation at a "fancy" restaurant everyone had hyped up for days. We arrived, full of excitement, only to be greeted by... burgers. Which, at that time in Bulgaria, were something you only found in McDonald's.

"Burgers?" I thought. "Is this a joke? So much excitement all day long about burgers?"

It may seem like a small thing, but it shows how cultural beliefs run deep.

Of course I could only share my thoughts on the burgers (and everything else) with Nasko, since I still spoke barely a few words of English. I love talking to people, and not understanding anything felt like an invisible wall keeping me out of sync with everything around me, even while surrounded by new friends. At first, Nasko translated, explaining things back and forth between me and the others. But eventually, he said, "You have to figure it out."

My frustration simmered. Every part of me yearned for comfort, but something deep inside reminded me that this was a challenge, and I shouldn't turn away.

One of our vanmates, Vlad, was from Russia. He was a straight shooter but always kind with me, asking how I was doing when Nasko wasn't around to answer. He had started encouraging me to use hand gestures to communicate.

Then he said, "Let your Russian language come back. Just speak and let's see what is going to come out."

Something clicked. Like water from a barely-used faucet, my rusty Russian from school started trickling back in. As I fumbled through sentences, Vlad was amused and patient, coaching me along. Somehow, between fragmented Russian and hand gestures, I found a bridge—a small one, but enough to connect.

That road trip brought me to a crossroads: either go back home or adapt, learn, and thrive. As my father would say, no matter what, you can always find a way. Generational cycles can be a good thing sometimes.

The future was wide open, and though I could barely

see my way through it, I felt like I belonged somewhere. Maybe this world, with all its differences, could become my own, if I was willing to rise to the challenge.

In those days of unfamiliar faces, noisy streets, and endless discoveries, a piece of me found the courage to start anew.

*"When someone tells you*

*'That's impossible'*

*remember that they're
talking about their own
possibilities,
not your limitations.*

*Unknown*

# CHAPTER 14

# Home

Still, for the next three months, I returned to Bulgaria every single day.

I'd wake up in Nasko's studio apartment in Urbana-Champagne, this totally unfamiliar place where even the air felt new. My bag in the closet was packed and ready to go. I'd think about the world I'd left behind, and ache quietly for the parts of me still lingering there, woven into its streets and the laughter of the people I had known for so long.

And I'd search for flights.

I ate bread with ham and cream cheese every day because they were the only things that tasted familiar. Even the Chinese food tasted wrong, like a pale reflection of the flavors I remembered from Bulgaria. And all those buffets, with their rows upon rows of food... mountains of food, yet nothing that felt remotely like the home-cooked meals I missed. It felt excessive, and I couldn't bring myself to enjoy it.

Actually, everything felt excessive.

The massive scale of it all in America! Even the shopping carts in the grocery store. Everything required so much effort–learning new streets, meeting new people–and I had no distractions. I couldn't even watch TV, since I didn't understand what was being said. I was afraid to go outside alone, so I would feed the squirrels until they began knocking on the window for nuts, and wait for Nasko to get home from school. When we did try to socialize, conversations felt like minefields of awkward silences and stumbled words. I didn't want to ask for help, preferring to muddle through on my own, even if it meant staying in the shadows.

So I kept my silence wrapped around me like a shield. I spent lonely hours on the internet, chatting with my friends back home, just like I used to chat with Nasko when we were apart. The irony wasn't lost on me: I'd spent years aching for Nasko across an ocean, and now that I finally had him, I was aching for everyone else.

But the thought of leaving Nasko, just as I'd gotten him back, pulled at me like a physical ache. I began to realize that I didn't just miss home, my parents, my brothers, my friends—I missed the person I had been in that place. I missed the girl who knew which streets to walk down, those routines felt natural, who belonged without question. I missed the spontaneous moments that didn't require planning, the certainty of being known, the comfort of being seen.

Being so desperately lonely while also drowning in so much love was a kind of feeling I couldn't justify, especially to Nasko. How do you tell someone you feel hollow when you're standing next to that person, and they fill your heart? I had so much love, it felt like it should have been enough. But love couldn't fill the void where home used to be. I was full and empty at the same time, and I didn't know which feeling was stronger.

Three months in, I was barely holding on. I would clutch desperately to the tiniest fragments of familiarity I could find like a child holding a blanket in the dark—chat conversations with friends back home, Bulgarian music playing on repeat, the comfort of my native language. But it wasn't enough. Something had to give, and I knew in my bones that if I didn't make a choice soon, it was going to be me. Should I go home, lose Nasko, and give up the five years of long distance relationship and the efforts that came with it, along with the life we were just about to start building? Or stay here, and lose everything else?

My dad had taught me to never give up, and to focus on what I could do best. So I started in a way that was most comfortable.

The comfort for my nationality is, of course, food.

I wanted to surprise Nasko with a home-cooked meal that would taste and smell like Bulgaria, like comfort, like the life we used to have. Something that would remind both of us why we were doing this. I still hadn't worked up the courage to leave the apartment by myself–I was paralyzed by the idea of getting lost in a place where I couldn't speak the language well enough to ask for help, where I didn't know the streets or the bus routes or even how to read the signs. But one morning, I couldn't stand it anymore. I had to prove to myself that I could at least try.

I left the house.

It sounds so insignificant, but it felt enormous. My hands shook. My heart raced. I paid obsessive attention to every street, every building, every tiny detail along the way, memorizing them while fighting the terror that I would never find my way back. But I found the grocery store. I bought the cabbage and chicken with fumbling hands and no English… and I made it back home. When I walked through our door, clutching those groceries with pride, I felt like I'd just climbed Mount Everest.

Standing taller, I took over the tiny kitchen, which was just a sink, a small cabinet, and a stove. I had never cooked here before, but I situated myself and got to work, peeling, slicing, and boiling, hoping to fill our apartment with a familiar warmth. When Nasko came back from school, he opened the door, sniffed, and said, "The whole building smells like home!"

His words were a second victory. My plan had worked! But when we sat down, he looked at his plate of chicken and cabbage, and my simple pasta dish. His brow furrowed.

"Why are we eating different things?"

"Well, I bought this cabbage as my mom suggested. But as it cooked, it just… disappeared!"

His face went blank for a second, and then I saw him try to hold back laughter. "Did you throw away the outer leaves of the cabbage?"

"Of course!" I was annoyed but also a tiny bit amused.

"Show me."

I dug through the garbage and pulled out the discarded leaves. Nasko began to laugh uncontrollably. "This isn't cabbage! This is iceberg lettuce!"

I was stunned. I had spent nearly two hours cooking lettuce.

We started to laugh together. It was absurd, but it sparked something new in me: a curiosity to learn and experiment. I became fascinated by the differences in ingredients and how each had its own qualities. I wanted to know everything about cooking, especially spices, which would later become my secret weapon. That evening with the "iceberg cabbage" was the beginning of an unexpected culinary journey, one that made this new country feel a bit more like home.

We couldn't see it happening in real time, but through my daily cycle of leaving and arriving, something had begun to unfold deep inside me: real, hard-earned, bone-deep resilience. With each step I took, with each small victory of not getting lost, of asking for help in broken English, of surviving another day in a place that had felt impossible to survive, the ache that had been crushing me began, imperceptibly, to soften. The homesickness became something I could carry instead of something that was crushing me. And this new world—this terrifying, unwelcoming place—started holding pieces of me, too. A familiar route to the store... a cashier who smiled at me.. a street I could navigate without panic. I was becoming someone new without realizing the old me was slowly letting go.

And since Nasko and I had no norms, since we were no longer surrounded by our old culture, and didn't yet know our new one, there was no one around us to expect anything of us. There were no boundaries and no traditions. The only source of light was our love for each other, a symbol of the small world we started to build together.

One day, although I couldn't have known it then, I woke up and realized I was no longer arriving.

I was home.

101

*"To be away from home
and yet find oneself everywhere at home;*

*to see the world,*

*to be at the center of the
world,*

*and yet remain hidden
from the world."*

*- Charles Baudelaire*

# CHAPTER 15

# Survive & Thrive

That summer, Nasko got an internship in Seattle. The company paid for his plane ticket and accommodations, but we couldn't afford to buy another ticket for me. We refused to spend the summer apart, so we found a solution: the company agreed to pay for gas instead of Nasko's plane ticket, and we would drive across the country together. Suddenly, what could have been another separation became an adventure. And I'd finally get to meet my friend Kristina in real life.

I had connected with Kristina during those first few impossible months in Urbana-Champaign. Sensing how much I was drowning in my strange new reality, my Bulgarian friends had connected me with other people scattered across the US; strangers who might understand what I was going through, who could offer a fragment of the normalcy I was starving for. Kristina in Seattle was one of them.

The connection between us was instant; so easy and natural it almost made me cry from relief. In a time when every interaction felt exhausting, when I was constantly translating myself just to exist, talking to Kristina felt effortless. She was there during those lonely hours when my friends back home were asleep, separated from me by time zones. When darkness pressed in and I had no one to turn to, Kristina became my anchor. And knowing I'd actually get to meet her, that I'd have a friend waiting for me in this next chapter, was the first thing that made the move feel less terrifying and more like possibility.

I also got a part-time job at Blockbuster.

For those of you born after the nineties, Blockbuster is like Netflix, but an actual store where you go inside and pay to rent a physical DVD or VHS[5] movie. I think the manager, Mark, took me on as a challenge. He was an incredibly patient man, and it felt like he genuinely wanted to help me learn to understand and speak. When there were no clients in the store, he would sit down with me and we'd practice together. He'd show me, tell me the word, sometimes describe it with a movement of hands or facial expression—pretty much the same way I later taught my kids to be bilingual.

He didn't have to do any of this. No one paid him extra to teach me English. Sometimes, he would send me home with a movie and a note. Nasko would read the note and

---

[5] See Notes – P 295

translate it to me. It would say something like,

"Watch the movie. Who is your favourite character? What are some phrases that stood out to you? Pay attention to the colors of the cars the characters drive."

The next day, we'd talk about the movie and what I'd learned. And of course, with my deeply ingrained sense of respect of–and fear for–"those in power", I studied as hard as I possibly could.

My first paycheck was barely enough to matter in practical terms but emotionally, it was everything. Holding it, I felt a surge of pride so fierce it brought tears to my eyes–in myself, in my resilience, in my refusal to give up. This was tangible proof that I could survive, even thrive, in a place where every interaction required courage I didn't know I had. I felt like I was contributing something meaningful to the world instead of just taking up space. And more than that, it ignited something inside me. If I could accomplish this much while stumbling through broken English, what could I achieve if I truly mastered the language? The possibilities felt limitless, and, for the first time, within my reach.

*

I finally met Kristina in person, which felt like reuniting with someone I'd known my whole life. She immediately introduced us to her parents, who, without hesitation, invited us to go camping with a huge group of Bulgarians. We had no camping gear, but some money. Kristina's dad took us straight to the camping supply store, and within an hour, we had a tent, sleeping bags, a cooler, and everything else we needed.

That camping trip made me feel at home in a way I hadn't felt since leaving Bulgaria. We found new friends who spoke our language and understood our story. Life was starting to feel almost normal again, like the life I'd had back home. I felt like I could breathe for the first time in months.

But we were so close to the end. Nasko's internship was almost over, and we'd have to head back to Urbana-Champaign for him to complete his degree. The thought of leaving was crushing, but we knew we'd return, as Nasko was offered a full-time job to start the following year, after he completed his degree. We even left our camping gear at Kristina's house as proof of our commitment, as a physical promise that Seattle wasn't goodbye—it was a "see you soon".

*

When we returned to Urbana-Champaign in the fall, I enrolled in an English as a Second Language (ESL[6]) class and started searching for a job at a nail salon. Nasko had to come with me for the interviews so he could translate.

At the first salon we went to, they put me to the test right away, working on a client. Nasko waited patiently while I filed and polished away. But as soon as we left, he

---

[6] See Notes – p.295

said,

"Even if they call you back, you should not work here. There are video cameras everywhere, which means that they don't trust their workers."

I was so desperate for a job I wouldn't have minded such a thing, but Nasko isn't usually overly cautious. His insistence surprised me, so I trusted him.

The next experience was at The John George Salon, a sleek, luxurious place with a whole gamut of beauty offerings. It had a huge glass facade and tons of natural light, with a centre island that was adorned with fresh flowers. The walls were lined with oversized mirrors, where you could watch the reflections of eleven expert hairdressers at work. Beyond the hairdressers were the nail technicians, with a half-wall beyond that for privacy for the clients getting pedicures.

The owner, Stacy, was a petite American lady with big blond hair and a bigger smile.

"Diana recently moved to the States," Nasko explained, when he introduced us. "Although she doesn't yet speak perfect English, she's looking for a job. She can do manicures, pedicures, full sets of acrylics, and nail art. She's really good at drawing."

Stacey raised a perfectly-shaped eyebrow. "Drawing on nails?"

"Yes. We brought you some samples. She's hardworking and very ethical. If you show her how you want things done, she'll do it."

Stacey looked over my samples, then looked at Nasko and I.

All she asked was, "When can you start?"

*"Growth is uncomfortable; you have to embrace the discomfort if you want to expand"*

*– Jonathan Majors*

# CHAPTER 16

# New Culture

Stacey believed in me without knowing me, something I'd never experienced before. And she gave me a flexible schedule so I could attend my ESL classes.

Soon, she started transferring her own clients to me. One night, I came home and asked Nasko, "All of Stacey's clients gave me extra money today. Why are they giving me money when they already paid for this service?"

"Wow! This is a tip," Nasko explained. "They must really like what you did for them."

"One lady handed me as much as her service cost—and she seemed happy to!"

"They do that when they receive good service. You impressed her a lot!"

Another night, I returned to tell him that I'd just met a woman who had four ex-husbands. I was stunned.

"How many ex-husbands can you have in America?" I

asked.

Nasko grinned. "As many as you want!"

I had more to learn than I possibly could have imagined.

Beyond the professional hum of scissors and quiet conversations, was the kitchen. For me, this was the heart of The John George, where the true magic happened. In this hidden retreat, we gathered for breaks, sharing stories and home-cooked potluck dishes.

As was my way, I'd try to compensate for not knowing the language by being extra vigilant. I paid attention to everything and everyone, absorbing every interaction and every conversation, trying to learn the culture, the norms, and how I could fit in. Meanwhile, everyone who worked there took it on as a challenge to teach me to speak English, and especially English slang. They helped me with homework. They made me want to speak up even when I couldn't, and got me to answer the phone. They empowered me to never give up in a time when I was struggling. Their encouragement meant so much to me. While I was so far from my home and my parents, these women had front seats to my struggles. They had witnessed my growth, and were able to see me for who I was.

They all have a very special place in my heart.

Many Bulgarians at that time (and still today) believed that if you send your kid outside of the country, they'll have a better chance to succeed. I disagree. Going to another part of the world is not what makes a person thrive. Success is in us. If you are willing to get up whenever you fall, and keep on going, I believe you can be successful no matter where you are.

I also believe that many immigrants are successful away from their country because they are alone. We don't have anyone to judge us or hold us back and talk us out of challenges before we even get started. Success is often taken from us by well-meaning friends, family members, or a community who don't share our vision. For me, successful people (and I don't just mean financially) are the ones who do the work even when no one is watching and no one understands them.

They are the ones with the drive to get up no matter how many times they fall.

Until, of course, they fall one time too many.

*"Real intimacy isn't built in the bedrooms but in conversations where your raw thoughts, fears, and truths are met with love, patience, and a desire to understand."*

*- Steve De'lano Garcia*

# CHAPTER 17

# Move

The following year, after Nasko graduated, we packed up our belongings and moved there–another small restart, but this time, one I was looking forward to. We'd made so many Bulgarian friends there it almost felt like we were going back home.

And the ladies at the salon had prepared me well for my next step.

"You've come a long way," one said. "Your English is good now. You don't have to be perfect at it. Remember, intelligent people will find a way to understand you, regardless of your accent."

I wanted to return to interior design, and I had to start somewhere, so I found a job in a high-end furniture store. To my surprise, my Russian skills suddenly came in handy–the wealthy Russian community in Bellevue was thrilled to shop with me. My manager was less thrilled when they would come in with bags of cash and the entire store staff would gather to count the money.

With Nasko and I both gainfully employed, and the economy being such that they gave loans to anyone with a pulse, we were able to buy our first piece of real estate: a condo.

Credit had existed in communist times in Bulgaria, but it was generally controlled by the state. If you wanted something, you usually saved and saved until you could buy it outright. Homes were often passed down from parents to kids, or parents would build houses with several stories so that their kids' families could move in down the line.

We didn't even have to make a down payment on our first home. I was so anxious, I didn't sleep for a month.

But I was also beside myself with awe. Almost everything in our new place was the opposite of the Soviet-style buildings I was used to. The building was modern, and the condo was remodeled and freshly painted—and *carpeted*! It had a view of the lake and was close to a park. The complex had two tennis courts, a small gym, and a pool. We couldn't afford any furniture at first, so we slept on an old mattress with moving boxes as nightstands. Still: having grown up sharing a two-bedroom apartment with two parents, two brothers and a grandma, I felt like I was living in a mansion.

And yet apparently, in my mansion, I belonged in the kitchen.

I worked Saturdays and Sundays at the furniture store, and had Wednesdays and Thursdays off. Nasko worked weekdays and had weekends free. He hated having nothing to do on weekends while I was gone, so he found himself a hobby: photography. He bought a camera and started exploring Seattle with it, capturing the city in ways I was too exhausted to see. He'd come home Saturday evenings with memory cards full of images: the Space Needle at sunset, strangers at the market, rain-soaked streets reflecting neon lights.

By the time I'd dragged myself home from work, my feet aching from showing furniture all day, the apartment would be quiet except for the clicking of his mouse. He'd be glued to the computer, absorbed in editing his photos, while I moved through the kitchen, chopping onions, boiling water. In our culture, women were expected to cook, clean, serve, wash clothes and dishes—essentially to do all the housework while the men went out and provided. Although most Bulgarian women now worked outside of the house, this pattern had hung on... and so had the one where women were supposed to stay quiet and not voice their opinions. Men still felt that they could come home, sit on the couch, wait to be served a cold drink, and sometimes give thoughtful directions about how things should be done.

But I hadn't grown up that way. My dad adored women and treated them with respect. There was no hierarchy in my home: if he wanted something from the kitchen, he got it himself. Both my parents took care of the housework when they were around, and when they weren't, my brothers and I did our equal share. My dad had made sure I had all the skills I needed so that I would not depend on anyone, or allow anyone to boss me around.

Since there had been little time for feelings in my family growing up, I knew that if I wanted something, I had to speak up and be direct. I usually wanted us to resolve things on the spot, while Nasko preferred to avoid conflicts and discuss them later (i.e. hoping whatever it was would be forgotten).

One night, I just blurted out.

"I'm tired of preparing and cooking everything while you edit photos on the computer."

He mumbled something about how important his pictures were and ignored me.

I brought it up again.

He brushed me off again.

My patience began to boil over. To me, this wasn't a way of resolving problems. It was a way of making them grow.

"I am not a housekeeper," I said, "and I'm definitely not your personal cook. I'm looking for a partner who will walk through life with me, not to be someone's mom. You can't just sit and expect me to serve you a meal."

He shrank back, his eyes fearful like a child caught in a lie, and looked down at his hands, as if they might hold the answer.

After a few moments, he said, "But I don't know what to do."

"I don't either," I said. "But it might be easier if we figure it out together."

It took almost a year of me continuing to remind him that if we were going to be equals in this relationship, we had to show up as a team, but we began to figure it out. We learned how to do as much or as little housework as felt good for us to co-exist. He started surprising me with dinner when I came home. We made time to go shopping together, and I encouraged him to participate in making decisions on what we needed to make our place a home, like furniture, art, plants. It felt important that we were invested together, rather than me picking everything and him coming home to a place he had no attachment to.

We didn't realize that this experience was going to become foundational for us. We felt more connected because we were both equally involved, and this connection became crucial when we had kids, especially when they started trying out different ways to convince us individually of what they wanted. We learned to agree that there's no such thing as overcommunicating, and began constantly discussing, disagreeing, and meeting in a place that makes sense for us both.

> *"We have all known the
> long loneliness and we
> have learned that the only
> solution is love and that
> love comes with commu-
> nity,"*
>
> *- Dorothy Day*

# CHAPTER 18

# Growth

The Bulgarian community in Seattle had become our lifeline. But there was one couple we connected with in a way that felt less like friendship and more like finding family. Niki was twenty-five years older than us and Reny, fifteen. But the age gap never mattered. From the first time we met them, on a camping trip, something clicked. They saw us for who we really were—young, passionate, occasionally naive, stumbling through building a life in a foreign country—and instead of judging us, they guided us. They became the parents we both needed at the moment in our lives we needed them most.

We spent all our free time with them. They opened their lives to us, inviting us to their home, including us in their backyard barbecues and their impromptu dinners. They treated us like our struggles were valid; like our dreams were worth pursuing. We'd visit their pizza restaurant and they would sit with us and advise us on our latest trials and tribulations. Niki's calm, grounded presence made us feel safe just being in the room with him, and Reny countered his quiet wisdom with her fiery energy and unstoppable force, always planning the next adventure.

We spent so much time together that talking about marriage became a running joke.

"So when are you two finally getting hitched?" Reny would tease, refilling our wine glasses. "What's taking so long?"

I had already proposed to Nasko on several occasions. He never took me seriously. In our culture, of course, men proposed.

"I need to figure it out," he'd say.

"Figure out what? I don't want a ring. You know that."

I don't think either of us gave these conversations that much weight. We just assumed we'd get married eventually.

So our answer to Reny was along the same theme, each time.

"We're not ready," I'd say, or, "Nasko isn't ready."

One night, after much wine, she got serious.

"You know what? If not having a best man and maid of honor is what's stopping you, consider it solved. We volunteer." She gestured between herself and Niki. "Now what's your excuse?"

We laughed, but there was something real underneath the joke. They weren't just offering to stand up at our wedding. They were saying, "We're here. We're your people. We've got you." And they were always there when we needed help, like when our car broke down, or we couldn't figure out some bureaucratic nightmare. But also, the harder kind of help: the honest truth, even when it wasn't comfortable. They told us what we needed to hear, not what we wanted to hear, but with so much love. One night, when I was sharing my new, vivid ideas about opening a Bulgarian restaurant, they both listened without interrupting. When I was done, Reny slammed her fist on the table.

"Over my dead body," she said. "The restaurant business is not for you. Sit down on your bottom and go back to school."

I was confused. They were successful restauranteurs—didn't she want the same for me? But I didn't push the issue. Remember, I'd been trained to show respect for people who were older than me, and to not question what they said. Communism taught us to never question our elders, our parents, or anyone professional like a doctor, a teacher or a lawyer. I had been imprinted with these rules.

Nasko's photography hobby grew into something more serious. He started taking classes, joining organized day trips with other photographers, spending hours studying composition and light. His camera became an extension of his body, always ready. And less than a year after buying that camera, he had his first show.

I'd never seen him so excited. He invested in everything—prints on special metallic paper that made the colors shimmer, high-quality frames with museum-grade glass. We spent countless evenings at the kitchen table, painstakingly choosing mat colors for each photo. He agonized over decisions that seemed small, but made all the difference.

The entire collection sold out on the opening weekend. I watched the disbelief wash over his face as the gallery owner placed red "sold" dots next to his photos, one by one. It was so much more than financial success—it was proof that his vision, his dedication, his countless hours of learning and practicing had created something real. That moment gave him the confidence to keep going, to see photography not just as a hobby but as something he could actually pursue.

Meanwhile, I could feel that I had gotten a little too comfortable at my furniture store job. I was earning good money (speaking Russian gained me a lot of clients) but I was unhappy in a way that felt urgent, like I was wasting time I'd never get back. The work had become monotonous and predictable, but what bothered me more than the repetition was the schedule. I still worked weekends while Nasko had them off. We were living together but existing in parallel universes. This wasn't the life I'd crossed an ocean to build.

At parties with our friends, the conversation always eventually turned to work. People would talk about their careers, their ambitions, their next moves, and I'd feel an ache—I wanted to grow, to have better opportunities, to be challenged in ways that mattered, just like my dad.

I knew I was capable of more.

So after Reni forcefully rejected my idea of opening a Bulgarian restaurant, I followed her advice. I went back to school, transferring my degrees from Bulgaria, jumping through bureaucratic hoops I didn't fully understand to take extra classes to fill gaps in the American system. I had no clear plan, no specific goal, just a bone-deep certainty that I needed to prepare myself for something different. I was building a foundation even though I couldn't see what I'd eventually construct on it.

It was only later that I learned how tough the restaurant business was—how you're always working because you're essentially always open.

I'm very grateful I did not take this path.

> **"Love doesn't make the**
> **world go 'round.**
>
> **Love is what makes the**
> **ride worthwhile."**
>
> *- Franklin P. Jones*

# CHAPTER 19

# Engaged

In May of that year, Nasko and I took the ferry to Blake Island, a small island in Puget Sound. We visited Tillicum Village, ate salmon cooked over an open fire, and wandered down to the beach. With Seattle's skyline behind us, it felt like a momentary escape from our work schedules, the apartment, the constant hustling just to get by.

The sandy beach was dotted with driftwood and smooth stones, and felt cool and soft on our feet. The air smelled like salt and pine. We both got quiet, just walking, breathing, existing together in a way we rarely got to anymore.

We sat down on a piece of driftwood at the beach, and Nasko turned to face me. There was something in his expression I couldn't quite read—anxiety, excitement, and fear.

"I have something to ask you," he said.

My heart started pounding.

He dropped to one knee, pulled a small ring box from his pocket, and asked me to marry him.

I couldn't speak. I just nodded, tears streaming down my face, while he slipped the ring onto my finger with shaking hands. We were almost levitating with happiness.

Later, on the ferry ride back, as we watched the sun drop toward the horizon, he confessed that he'd been carrying the ring for two weeks. He'd hidden it in the spare tire of the car, of all places, waiting for the right moment, my thoughts on rings echoing in his years. Every day, he'd wondered if today was the day.

Of course, we asked Niki and Reny to be our best man and maid of honor—not out of obligation, but because they were already playing those roles in our lives. They were the people who helped us become the adults we needed to be.

Reny smiled and immediately accepted, while Niki pulled us both into a hug and said, simply, "It would be an honor."

And of course, I lost the diamond in the ring a week later, and I never wore the thing again.

*

Shortly before we got engaged, my friend Maria had pulled me aside.

"I've had enough of watching you be miserable," she said. "I'm going to help you find another job."

Maria didn't just send me job postings or offer vague encouragement. She actively worked her network for me. She was introducing me to people who introduced me to other people.

Meanwhile, bubbling with excitement, I asked my bosses for time off from the furniture store for when we got married, a year from now. They refused. We were planning a big sale around that time, they said. They needed me there.

I couldn't believe they thought a sale was more important than someone's wedding. I said, "I quit," and walked out on the spot.

Thankfully, by that point, Maria and her friend Diana had lined up an interview at an architectural firm for me. All I knew about architecture was how to do the drawings and how to read them, but I prepared like mad, especially since I was unemployed. I gave the interview everything I had, and landed the job.

We got married in Bulgaria a year later in May, and then had a big party with all our friends in Chicago. After that, we had another wedding in Seattle. We basically celebrated for a month. Niki and Reny were at every single event.

And Nasko and I planned it all together, as a team.

*"Having a baby is a life-changer.*

*It gives you a whole other perspective on why you wake up every day."*

Taylor Hanson

# CHAPTER 20

# Roadmap

We'd gotten the jobs, we'd bought the house, we'd gotten married. We'd followed the roadmap that American society lays out for everyone.

Our plan was to delay having kids for a while, since we both really wanted to take time to travel. But soon after we got married, Nasko announced, "I think I'm ready to have a baby."

"Where's this coming from?" I asked, stunned. "What happened to all the travel and exploring we're going to do?"

"We'll just take the baby with us," he said, shrugging. "Plus, it might take time. So why wait?"

That December, while we were doing the paperwork and getting the required shots to go to India, the doctor mentioned that he couldn't vaccinate me if I was pregnant.

"Oh, she is," Nasko said, casually.

I thought he was joking. It felt like an out-of-character

overstep into my personal space, especially since I wasn't showing any signs of pregnancy. (Although I was very disconnected from my body at that time.)

"How would you know that? It's my body and I don't even know that."

The doctor looked back and forth between us.

"Let's solve this argument," he said.

He ordered some bloodwork right away. The lab technician must have been quite taken by our conversation, because we got the results back in 5 minutes, even though there were people before us in line.

"Girl," she said, "you are so pregnant."

Nasko was over the moon. I was in shock, but that quickly turned into elation.

And we went to India anyway.

***

The next expected step, of course, was to "buy a bigger house" (and also an SUV and lots of stuff). To be fair, the economy was changing rapidly, and we were worried that if we didn't buy a bigger home soon, we wouldn't be able to afford one. We had decided to start looking four months before I got pregnant, even though our mortgage would become even more of a stretch. (We skipped the SUV, though.)

Nothing felt right. The visits became robotic; just checking a box that we had seen a place. It took nine months of searching, but when we stepped inside our home, I felt a magical, inexplicable feeling of rightness. I stood at the entryway, knowing the feeling had nothing to do with logic.

The kitchen was so much bigger than anything we'd had before, with long stretches of counter space, and cabinets with actual storage. I could picture it filled with friends gathered around while I cooked, the smell of Bulgarian food filling the space, ingredients spread across the counters. There was an entire playroom dedicated to the beautiful chaos of childhood. I imagined toys scattered across the floor, art projects covering the table, and laughter echoing off the walls... space for kids to be fully, joyfully themselves.

But the backyard sealed the deal. Large and open, with grass and mature trees providing shade, and no neighbours facing us, perfect for summer barbecues with our Bulgarian friends, kids running wild, maybe a garden where I could grow tomatoes and peppers. This wasn't just a house. This was where we'd build our life.

I was five months pregnant when we moved in. Our new neighbors came over immediately to welcome us with wine and gifts. We decided to host a small housewarming BBQ to get to know them.

Rocky, a kind, big-hearted veteran who lived across the street, said, "I'm retired. I'm always home. You can count on me to look after the baby anytime you need to shower."

We thanked him, but were confused. What did he mean? The baby would be sleeping most of the time. I'd have plenty of time to do housework, cook, and, obviously, wash myself.

Then, at my baby shower, everyone kept saying, "Remember, when that baby sleeps, you drop everything and sleep too."

It felt like everyone was repeating the same joke. Remember, we were barely adults ourselves– the youngest people in our prenatal classes by at least 10 years.

"Babies eat, they sleep, and they poop," we thought. "That's it. Like in the movies!"
And then, Daniel was born.

# Generational Resilience

*"Parenting is the easiest thing in the world to have an opinion about*

*and*

*the hardest thing in the world to do"*

*- Matt Walsh*

# CHAPTER 21

# Surviving

After I gave birth, the nurses brought me a hospital-grade pump to help with my breastmilk. It felt like it was going to suck my brain out of my head.

Still, no milk came.

Daniel was crying—a lot. Formula saved us for a few days, and while I fully respect that breastfeeding is a personal choice, I was determined to do so, and ready to do anything to make it happen.

A few days, a lot of hot showers, some positive thinking, and massive doses of support from our Bulgarian neighbor Boryana later, the milk started coming.

But Daniel continued to scream.

My mother-in-law stayed with us for a couple of weeks. She took care of us while we took care of the baby as best we could based on what we knew. He kept screaming. We visited several pediatricians and lactation specialists. One doctor told us that our little boy was tongue-tied. Of course, we had to ask what this meant.

"It means he can't stick his tongue out far enough to breastfeed. Don't worry, he'll outgrow it. The tissue will stretch as breastfeeding goes on."

That made sense to us, so we didn't ask about other options. Remember: to us, doctors were akin to gods. You don't question them. And there was my family legacy: don't pause and reflect, you brush yourself off and keep on going.

The lactation specialist said, "Your baby is working so hard to get milk that he's getting tired more quickly and having shorter sleeps because he isn't getting enough food."

So we started supplementing by feeding him with a tube, but he still had to suck the milk that I had to pump before that. They recommended we follow a strict schedule of feeding him every three hours.

Sleep deprivation is no joke. It limits what your brain is able to do. Our home was in chaos, with days and nights merging into one: pump, wake up the baby, change the baby, feed the baby, clean all the pumping equipment, short sleep, repeat. We were in survival mode, just trying to make it to the next feeding. No one talks about these parts of having a baby (except our neighbors and friends, of course, who did try their best to warn us).

As exhausted as we were, we decided to work with what was in our control. We figured out that no one had the right to wake up a sleeping baby, even though the pediatricians had recommended feeding him every three hours.

"Let's let him sleep," Nasko said. "We'll feed him when he wakes up on his own."

The night we started following Daniel's schedule was the first night since he was born that we slept for five or six hours. It felt like a miracle, but the whole routine of supplemental feeding was still exhausting. We survived two more weeks, and then learned that there was another option: to cut the short lingual frenulum. Why had no one told us this before? Or maybe someone had, but we were too exhausted to listen.

There are no blood vessels in the tongue region. It's just a membrane, but cutting it is technically "surgery", which only certain doctors do since surgery on babies can come with a bunch of complications. We managed to escalate the issue to emergency, and in a few days, our world changed.

Our boy breastfed—really breastfed, without screaming—and then slept for five straight hours straight. When I woke up, I couldn't believe it. I checked multiple times to see if he was still breathing. I checked the clock three times, convinced it was broken.

We could function again.

We began to understand that although they are so new to this world, babies sometimes know better than us what they need. They are our teachers, and our work, as parents, was to listen. The better listeners we became, the more we would learn that would enrich all of our lives. This taught us to go with our gut feeling to resolve issues as soon as possible, regardless of what other people advised.

141

*"If parenthood came with GPS, it would mostly just say,... 'recalculating."*

*- Simon Holland*

# CHAPTER 22

# Fairy Tales

Finally, we were able to enjoy our new family of three.

I took three months of maternity leave and was allowed to work from home for the next three, which was rare. Like my Blockbuster boss and Stacey at John George, my boss at the architecture firm, Carl, was another angel. (I did learn later that Carl hired foreigners almost exclusively. He was transparent about why: because we worked harder, and never complained–a profile I certainly fit to.)

When it was time to return to the office, Nasko, Daniel and I piled into the car and went to register at the daycare near my work. They welcomed us in with open arms.

"I would like my son to attend your daycare," I told the principal.

"Absolutely. When did you sign him up?"

"Oh no, we haven't done that yet. That's why we're here today."

The woman looked at me apologetically. "That might be a problem. We're at full capacity. And we have an 18-month waiting list."

I felt like I'd been hit by a train.

"An... 18-month waiting list?"

"Yes."

"So if I had signed him up the moment I discovered I was pregnant, you still wouldn't be able to take him now?"

"Correct. I understand how confusing that is."

It was another one of the many ideas from my old life I still held onto. In Bulgaria, when it's time for daycare, you sign your kid up for daycare. How in god's name did American parents do anything?

We called every daycare in our area. Each one had a similarly long waiting list. My parents were far away and working, and Nasko's were in Chicago and also working. It felt like a puzzle with no solution, and we were out of time.

We ended up going with the only plan we could think of: each morning, I'd head to work at 4:30am, driving through quiet streets as the city was barely waking up. I'd work until noon, then rush home. Nasko would hand me Daniel in the garage in what became known as the Baby Switch-Off. These were our only moments to connect, and for Nasko to hurriedly update me on feedings and diaper changes.

Then he'd race to work and stay until 11pm.

Talk about the American dream. I still shudder just thinking about it.

We ran this relay race every day. I'd spend the afternoon caring for Daniel, cleaning, washing, and cooking, and finding fleeting moments of rest before we started the evening routine. At midnight, Nasko would return home, worn out but grateful, and I would be fast asleep. We were a seamless tag team bound by love and necessity. Luckily, both of our employers were supportive.

But the stress took its toll. By the second or third weekend, we met up with some friends. We must have looked pretty bad, because they expressed concern for our "condition". One even decided to step in and help us. Vania would come in the morning so Nasko could go to work during regular hours, while I continued on the same early schedule. This gave us the opportunity to both be at home for dinner and to have a slightly more normal life.

Becoming a parent is a monumental life change that can overwhelm even the most well-prepared people, and we were not prepared at all. But looking back, I also appreciate how unprepared we were. In Bulgaria, and especially in communist times, when you had a child, you had people around you who could help (and daycare was always available). Being new parents in America felt like being in the middle of the sea on a tiny boat with a constant storm. If we had known how hard it would be, we might not have proceeded.

Maybe that's why we believe in fairytales. They give us hope and move us forward. Challenges are easier to overcome when we take them one at a time.
As we were about to find out.

*"Spending time with chil-
dren
is more important
than
spending money on chil-
dren."*

*- Anthony -Douglas Williams*

# CHAPTER 23

# The Crash

We "convinced" my grandmother to come to the US from Bulgaria for six months and help us out. Not that it took much convincing. My 69-year old grandma, who had never left the country or been on a plane, jumped to help us. She was the kind of person who cares for everyone else before herself, which is another legacy I inherited quite nicely. But at the time, it felt like some kind of miracle.

My grandma spent all Daniel's waking hours on the floor with him, letting him know that there was a reliable adult there for him and that he was loved and cared for, just as she had for my brothers and me. She was 100% devoted to him. We had a lot of toys (far too many) that made sounds and noises. One day, I noticed that some of them had been turned off, and I asked her why.

"Oh, they are too annoying and too loud," she said.

I told her that these were essential noises that Daniel needed to learn. She never turned those toys off again.

I became fascinated by Daniel's persistence in learning to crawl, first backwards, then forwards. He kept going until he succeeded. Babies are so resilient. Everything is possible, and they keep trying until they achieve it.

When I came home from work, my grandma would bring me up to speed on what new thing he'd done that day.

"Look, he learned how to flip himself over!"

"He pushed himself onto his knee for the first time!"

"He stood up on his legs!"

She was so excited about each new achievement and so eager to share them all with me. Meanwhile, I felt increasingly awful to be missing moments that we would never get back. I promised myself that when we had a second child, I would not miss any of these milestones.

Then, fall of 2008 came, and the US economy crashed.

Commercial architecture was one of the first fields to get hit. At my work, we switched to residential, accommodating entitled clients who would call in with minute changes every day... until that dried out, too. No one was building anything. I held on to the kind of hope I had later on when my father was dying, that something would change, even though people were already being laid off at my office. My boss, Carl, paid us out of pocket until the beginning of 2009. Then I got laid off. Two months later, in March of 2009, the economy hit rock bottom.

When you buy a house as a couple in America, you assume you will continue to have two incomes to keep paying for it. Now, I felt like I was reliving my parents' story. The money was gone. The fear of losing our house was enormous. The responsibilities of having a newborn were inescapable.

My parents had risen up again, over and over. But they never let us in on the lesson. It was like watching a magic trick—everything falling apart, then suddenly fixed. There were no lessons in budgeting, no talks about saving or investing, no conversations about navigating the inevitable downturns of money. The unspoken rule was just to endure.

Maybe they were too caught up in surviving to even think about teaching us. Maybe they thought that by bouncing back again and again, they were showing us everything we needed to know. But resilience alone isn't enough. We needed the tools, the knowledge, and the understanding of how to break free from that cycle of loss and recovery.

When I got laid off, just like that day in my parents' kitchen when they learned all their money was gone, I became frozen—and stayed that way for two weeks. I existed like a ghost, doing what needed to be done, spiralling through all the phases of grief. Why was this happening to me? This was not fair! How were we going to live off one income? IIow could this happen? We lived in America now! Like that fact was going to save us.

I started applying for jobs in order to qualify for unemployment. Once I saw that no one was hiring, I got the bigger picture, that I wasn't the only one affected by this. Everything from the time in my life that the banks collapsed came flooding back once agin: the feeling of scarcity, the going into freeze mode. Both of us just took care of whatever we could without a real conversation or strategy, but after a couple of weeks, I remembered: we were in charge here. We needed to be part of the solution.

Getting up and brushing ourselves off without reflecting wasn't going to cut it this time.

Nothing about the situation could be changed, so we figured we might as well take the best parts of it, refocus, figure out how to save our house, and move forward. Together, we looked out our finances and cut as many expenses as possible. Because I had such a strong belief that money was "temporary", I'd never had the urge to understand compound interest, taxes, or investments. Now, I was too preoccupied with Daniel and had no bandwidth to learn, whereas Nasko's sense of responsibility about being a new dad seemed to kick in instinctively. He started learning about the stock market. We figured out that we could actually live within our means. Plus, now I got to stay home with Daniel, who was already a year old.

Eventually, despite it appearing from the outside to be the most insane decision possible, we decided to have our second child at that time. We didn't know how long this situation of me being off work would last, and more importantly, we realized there was never going to be a "right time". Something would always be a "problem". But problems always pass. The economy always changes. Having lived through so much in Bulgaria, I knew, even if it was subconsciously, that things would shift again.

"We'll eat bread and salt if we have to," I told Nasko, repeating a cultural phrase we'd grown up with.

I was determined to be at home with our second child, no matter what.

And those toys my grandma had briefly complained about? Turns out they were extremely loud and very annoying. She had sacrificed even this for me.

As soon as I started staying home with Daniel, they never got turned on again.

*"The sun always shines
above the clouds"*
*- Paul Davis*

# CHAPTER 24

# The Scare

Before I learned I was pregnant with our second child, I had a very specific desire: we had a son, now I wanted a daughter.

Of course, this was at a time when my understanding of gender was still binary. I even "interviewed" a bunch of different people about what they hoped for, and they all reported the same—one of each. It made me wonder if we all somehow had the same wish; that same fairytale view on life.

I asked my OBGYN, "Is there a recipe to have a girl?"

He smiled politely. "If there were," he said, "I wouldn't have three boys."

He added that they could send the sperm and egg to a lab in California, where they'd spin and wash them and return only the girl ones to us. But I wasn't that desperate.

I just wanted to make sure I wasn't missing out on some natural way of doing things.

"I've read a lot about food restrictions and poses and wanted to see if you have any suggestions that work," I pressed.

He refrained from commenting and continued with the exam.

Despite his reservations, I embarked on my quest, exploring every old wives' tale, remedy, pose, or suggestion I came across. The time of conceiving is apparently important, as are the acidity of the food you eat, what you drink, how much you eat, and when. We tried it all.

I got pregnant again in March of 2009. I started having contractions at 17 weeks, so my OBGYN put me on bedrest. This felt impossible with a toddler at home, but I had no choice. Two of my neighbours, Vania (who was pregnant with twins) and Elena would come over and entertain Daniel and Elena's baby while I lay on the couch.

The contractions slowed a few weeks later, and I was allowed to move, but with limitations.

"You can't pick Daniel up, or help him climb," my doctor instructed me. It felt like yet another impossible ask— like I'd just gotten up, only to be knocked down again.

"You know I have a toddler at home, whom you delivered, right?" I asked the doctor. "He still exists."

He responded, kindly, that this was my challenge to resolve.

Like a lot of new moms, I had taken my role very seriously. As soon as I heard the call – "Mama, help!" – I'd run. I picked him up and put him in his car seat. I helped him climb the stairs to the slide at the playground, then held him so he didn't bump his head when he slid down. I played with him in the sandbox instead of letting him play with other kids.

But under these new restrictions, my eyes opened to how dependent I had let Daniel become on me. I had been making sure he was safe to the point that I had actually put him in danger by not allowing him to experience the "mistakes" he'd need to develop the skills he would need to get through life. I'd been so hooked on giving him all the attention and presence I hadn't gotten from my parents, I hadn't given him any space at all.

Changing this dynamic was frustrating for both of us at the beginning. I told him, "You're a big boy now. Show me how you can climb into your carseat."

"No!" he wailed. "Mama, help!"

It broke my heart, but I had no choice.

"You can do it!" I encouraged him. "I know you can."

In no time, he learned how to climb in and out of the car and sit in his car seat. I just buckled him in. He stopped expecting me to participate in all of his activities, all the time. He learned how to slide without me, and without bumping his head. He learned how to climb the stairs.

His new catchphrase became, "I can."

My helicopter parenting had not been limited to outdoor play and climbing into the car seat. I had been taking him to an art class where the children were meant to explore and make a mess with paint.

"This is messy," he'd told me. "Can I have a brush?"

So instead of using his fingers like the other children were doing, I taught him how to paint with a brush. Yes, this advanced his painting skills, but it also restricted his ability to explore the different textures and surfaces of the paint. He was at the perfect age for discovery. Kids learn through using all of their senses. Touch is very important at that age, as they discover different textures

I'd been stuck on teaching him "the right" way of doing things. *We paint with a brush. We eat with a fork."* I quickly realized that there was all the time in the world for that sort of behaviour (as any of us raised by parents even vaguely concerned about table manners know). While my brothers and I had had a lot of freedom, we were never allowed to come home muddy. My parents would give us a lecture if we did, but our friends received far worse punishments.

I wasn't allowing Daniel to be a kid. I was so afraid he might miss some major developmental milestone that I was robbing him of one of the most precious times in his life; one, that he would never get back.

So I cranked up our mess-making activities at home. We used our hands to paint. We painted with foam in the bathtub. We coloured the water and the foam and drew with special crayons on the tiles. He played with sand and dirt, dug for worms in the backyard, and then measured them. We walked in the rain without an umbrella.

"Danny," I said, one day, "let's see which puddle will make the biggest splash."

"Mama first!" he cried out, delighted.

The two of us went home soaking wet, and so happy.

As Thomas Froese said, "Prepare the child for the road, not the road for the child."

***

One afternoon, when I was 19 weeks pregnant with our second baby, our nurse called.

"Hi Didi. Your lab results have returned, and they

don't look good."

The room started to spin.

"What do you mean, 'they don't look good'?"

"They are very elevated."

"Wh...what does that mean?"

"When results are this high, there's a big chance that your baby will have Down's syndrome."

In that moment, for me, everything stopped. I listened without understanding as the nurse's voice echoed somewhere in the background. Tears came. My stomach twisted in pain, and I slumped down to the floor. When I finally hung up with the nurse, I called Nasko. Through gasps and broken words, I managed something like, "T-t-t-h-h-h-e l-l-l-a-a-b r-e-s-u-l-t-s a-r-e n-o-t g-o-o-d. Something's wrong... I don't know what to do."

"I'm having a hard time understanding you," he said. "How about you hang up and I call the nurse?"

I must acknowledge that this was a knee-jerk reaction based on my cultural conditioning. It was not thought out or, more importantly, informed. I have nothing but respect for individuals with Down syndrome and their families, but at that time, all we knew from our upbringing was that this was bad news. In Bulgaria, during communist times, if a child even misbehaved in school for a prolonged period of time, they were sent to a special school for "correction", which brought shame upon the whole family. Everyone would ignore the child from then on. If a child failed at school, no matter what grade they were in, they repeated that grade over and over until they passed, and they were sent to a different school for "those kinds of students" to do so. Of course there were special needs children in Bulgaria, but, especially during communist times, they were rarely seen. You didn't see blind people in the streets, or people with wheelchairs. They simply "did not exist".

And none of this was openly discussed. It was universally accepted in our culture. To this day, many Bulgarians don't even believe in therapy, claiming it is for the "weak".

Nasko called the nurse, then dropped everything and rushed home. For the days and nights that followed, it felt like the walls were closing in on us. We moved like zombies. Our hearts ached under the weight of the stories we were telling ourselves. The conversations with the medical staff rang in our ears. Somehow, eventually, we managed to lean into the pain instead of resisting it, and imperceptibly, it began to soften. Everything started to become more fluid, and we were able to figure out the next step.

We decided not to accept–yet–what we had been told.

Six days after the call, we met with a counselor. My mind was frozen in fear, but Nasko stayed alert and focused. He listened to her rattle off different numbers and statistics until she paused and stepped out of the office to get something. Nasko took the little circles they use, based on a woman's cycle, to predict a baby's due date. We knew exactly when our baby was conceived. He played with those circles for a bit.

When the counselor returned, he asked, "What if the due date given to us is wrong by a week?"

"Let me see." She tapped something out on her keyboard. "If the due date is off by a week... then the lab results are in a normal range."

Nasko turned to me. "Our baby doesn't have Down's syndrome," he said. "The due date they have is wrong by a week."

I stared at him. "How do you know?"

Patiently, he explained it again. It felt like a window had opened and a cool breeze had swept into the room.

We returned to the clinic for the ultrasound, and I felt a familiar twinge of apprehension. But as we settled into the room and faced the technician, I knew we had to answer for ourselves. We decided to focus on what mattered: our family, our values, and the love we held for the life growing within me.

"Are you ready to face whatever might come?" the technician asked.

We looked at each other, took a deep breath, and nodded. She paused.

"Would you like to know the sex of your baby?"

"Yes, we want to know!" we answered in unison.

"Congratulations! It looks like you will be having a girl."

We were so happy. Determined to move forward, the next step was the amniocentesis test, which the only way we could know 100% if our baby carried this genetic condition.

Time stood still in the days that followed. All we could do was wait and hold onto each other.

Then the nurse called. "Didi, the results are in. Your baby does not have Down syndrome, and it is confirmed that she is a girl."

The sex of my child had become totally unimportant to me during this process, but now, two wishes had been granted.

I burst into tears.

I'm certain that there are as many possible ways one can go as there are parents out there. And to this day, we stand by what choices we made in those moments. But so much of what we endured in those weeks could have been avoided if the system had taken a bit more time and care. If we weren't subject to a plethora of numbers that didn't acknowledge the humans involved; if I weren't just another patient among the many; just another pregnant woman moving through the medical system. There was no advice or no probing questions that might have alleviated our concerns sooner. They saw us from a one-dimensional approach.

And in the time that followed until Bella was born, I also gained a new understanding and awareness of the challenges and joys associated with raising a child with Down's syndrome. I continue to believe in the importance of acceptance, inclusion, and support within our communities.

I share this part of my journey not as a commentary on making a choice to continue with a pregnancy for any reason. I unequivocally support a woman's right to choose what happens with her body. But so much of what we endured in those weeks could have been avoided if the system had taken more time and more care. I had no idea how important this lesson would be a few years down the road.

*"When you lost your voice,
you lost the ability to
make sense of yourself"*

-Yōko Ogawa.

# CHAPTER 25

# Lost Voice

When Daniel started eating solid foods, he would have been happy to only eat prunes. But when he turned one, his grandparents and our friends started expecting him to have a more diverse diet. Food plays such a central role in Bulgarian society: beyond just nourishment, it's a symbol of hospitality, family bonds, and cultural pride. We have a deeply intertwined relationship with the struggle of not having enough food, mainly from when the communist regime collapsed.

We tried everything to get Daniel to eat. We gave him taste-improving drops that promised to make food more appealing. We tried appetite-awakening supplements that the pediatrician swore would work. Consultation after consultation, doctor after doctor, each one offering another theory; another solution; another way I was apparently failing my child. I was living by unspoken rules I'd never agreed to, carrying crushing guilt that wasn't even mine to carry: that I wasn't a good enough mother.

I fell into the trap of trying to meet everyone's expectations simultaneously, which was impossible. The cultural pressure wrapped itself around my throat so tightly I couldn't breathe. I don't recall my parents ever insisting we eat anything, although we certainly didn't have much to choose from but at daycare and preschool in Bulgaria, where lunch was always provided, you had to eat your soup and your main meal in order to get dessert. So I parroted the words my culture and every parenting book had told me to the kids: "You need to eat your vegetables before you can have dessert."

This, of course, makes vegetables seem like punishment and dessert like a reward.

I was so consumed with proving that my child wasn't "difficult" that I lost my own voice, and my own instincts. And still, nothing worked. Daniel would just sit there, tears streaming down his face, refusing to eat while I fought back my own tears of frustration. It wasn't pleasant for anyone—not for him, not for me, not for Nasko watching helplessly as I spiraled deeper into desperation and self-doubt.

And then one night, after another dinner that ended in tears and tension, I broke. I realized that everything I was doing was wrong, not because I was a bad mother, but because I was trying to be everyone else's version of a good mother, instead of just being Daniel's mother.

My son had a strong-willed, unwavering view of what

he wanted to put in his mouth. Nothing–no supplement, no bribe, no threat, no manipulation–was going to change that. Suddenly, through my exhaustion and frustration, a question emerged that should have been there from the beginning: what gives us the right to tell someone what they should eat? What gives anyone–me, the doctors, the grandparents, the parenting experts, society–the right to override Daniel's bodily autonomy, his innate understanding of what his body needs or doesn't need? I was trying so hard to force him to fit into everyone else's expectations that I couldn't see I was hurting us both.

Right then and there, I stopped. Daniel lived almost entirely on eggs and bread until he became a teenager (the eggs were inspired by Shrek, to whom I am grateful). People around us still dropped comments, and I never had the courage to stand up for our decision, so I simply kept to myself, although it hurt.

I still had a lot of room to grow.

*"Doing your best*

*is more important*

*than being the best"*

*- Zig Ziglar*

# CHAPTER 26

# Super Mom

After Bella was born, my creative side began to re-emerge. While searching for unique hair clips for her, I stumbled on the Japanese technique of Kanzashi[7], which is similar to origami but uses fabric to create flowers. I started to make these hair clips myself–first for Bella, then for friends.

One day, my friend Elena said, "I can't allow you to keep gifting those flowers any longer. You see that everyone wants them. Why don't you start selling them?"

So I did. And even though no one thought it would go anywhere, DidiArtCorner grew from hairpins to lapel pins, wedding bouquets, wristlets, and more. My flowers went to Elton John's Oscars afterparty–twice. I supplied

---

[7] See Notes – p.295

over 1000 weddings, and the governments of two countries.

You'd think that would have been enough for me. It wasn't. While I was launching my business, I came up with an idea that I should take the kids to every park in a 30-mile radius from our home. Every afternoon, I would fill the car with two bikes, a double stroller, a baby stroller for Bella's dolls, sand toys, every kind of ball in existence, rollersblades for Danny and myself, Danny's scooter, a beach umbrella, a picnic blanket, hats, a cooker, food, and a bag with extra clothes. Once we got there I would load and unload the car several times as the kids changed their minds about what they wanted to do. And I rarely asked for help. I did it all with love and care, but I didn't realize how much I was sacrificing my own self-care and putting the kids first.

Meanwhile, Nasko's 31st birthday rolled around, and I decided to make a cake shaped like a camera. I baked the sponge parts, froze them, and then created each part of the cake. I even printed a miniature photo to glue on the back like a screen. It took me two entire days, and the result was so realistic that it took time even for him to figure out that what was on the countertop was not a real camera.

But I never considered what all of it would cost me, energetically.

No one madde me do any of this. And I did all of that on top of taking care of everything else in the house, which

I'd started to do again since getting laid off from my job, despite all the time and effort Nasko and I had put in trying to become team players. I was feeding myself by making others around me feel special. I didn't have the awareness to know what it really was to be seen, or to be significant.

"Always do a million things at once. Don't stop to reflect or learn. Don't stop, period." That's what I learned from my parents. From society, I absorbed the glorified idea of being "supermom": overdoing, performing, and exhausting myself. In America, we only value what we can measure. How much money do you make? How many hours did you work this week? Can you put them on a spreadsheet? If you didn't do those things, did you take your kids to the park today? Did you cook dinner? Did you clean the house? These are considered less valuable. Maybe that's why so many women try to value themselves by overdoing everything.

My grandmother had sacrificed herself for her family. She never remarried. She dropped everything whenever we needed her. My parents had done it, the women around me in Bulgaria had done it, and

the women in America did it, too. I'm so grateful for what my grandma and parents gave up for me. I know it came from a place of love, but it meant putting themselves on the back burner, and barely (if it all) taking care of themselves.

And that is just not sustainable.

I'm still so proud of the success of my flowers, and so happy about how many people wear them. But all of this was just me trying to be another version of my dad.

*" When you travel with
children
you are giving something
that can never be taken
away...
experience exposure and a
way of life."*

*-Pamela Chandle*

# CHAPTER 27

# Parenting

In America, kids are supposed to have their own bedrooms. If your family has the means, that's just what's expected.. Even though I'd grown up sleeping in the same room with my two brothers and grandma, we once again followed expectations without questioning them.

But Bella and Daniel wanted to sleep in the same bed. We, following Western norms, insisted that everyone stayed in their own bed. They would wake up at different times of the night and come to our bedroom, and one of us would go back to one bedroom with one kid. We'd spend time with them until they fell back asleep, return to bed, and just be falling asleep when the other kid would come in with the same request. This happened two or three times a night.

Finally, we let them sleep together. OH MY, how we all slept. That first morning I saw both of my kids sound asleep, tangled up in each other's arms, my heart swelled. It wasn't worth trying to change their natural bond. Even when Bella snuck into our bed in the middle of the night, we welcomed it, cherishing all the closeness we could get. Our family nights became more peaceful, and everyone got the rest they needed. And I now understand that it was a way for them to bond; to get subconscious reassurance that they were not alone in a room that seemed big to a little person.

Listening to our kids–really listening–became a theme in our journey as parents. When Daniel was seven and Bella was five, when we spent five weeks living in Munich, Germany. It was our first time abroad long-term as a family, and it felt far outside our comfort zone, but we wanted to make the most of it.

"Mom," Daniel said, one day, "did you notice how many kids my age here are going to school by themselves? On the bus and in the trolleys? They go by themselves to the grocery store, too. Can I do that?"

I was stumped. Finally, I told him, "I can't let you go to school or the store alone in the US because it's illegal to let you wander by yourself at that young age."

*America,* I thought. *Home of the free.*

We talked about child services and the rules we must obey in the States. Daniel listened carefully.

"While we are here, can I go to the store by myself?" he asked.

Nasko and I talked about it later that night. Should we take the risk and give Daniel this experience, or keep him safe?

"The grocery store isn't a direct walk from our apartment," Nasko said. "Are you really going to be okay with him going alone? What about if he gets lost? He speaks no German. He has no phone."

The next night at dinner, Daniel asked again about going to the store. He was so intrigued about the German kids' independence. By then, we were prepared. We explained that we'd love to let him go alone, but since we were in a different country where we didn't speak the language, we would go to the store together and let him shop inside on his own.

He was thrilled.

The following day, as Nasko and I watched from the front window, Daniel went into the store. He got a carton of milk, waited patiently at the cash register, paid, and put it in his backpack. But as he reached for the change, the carton slipped out of his backpack and exploded on the floor. We both panicked, and I jumped to go inside and help him. Nasko stopped me.

"Let's stay here and let him have this experience without interfering."

We watched as one of the employees gave Daniel a paper towel. Daniel cleared up the milk, and went and got another carton. He got in line, and paid for it again, this time being extra cautious about zipping up his backpack.

He came outside, thrilled. He proudly explained what happened ("and I cleaned it all by myself!") We could see that he felt like he could conquer the world.

It was such a simple experience, but loaded with so much learning. In the US, someone would have come and cleaned up the milk for him, probably brought him another carton, and apologized. We saw how instantly allowing him to feel independent and own his journey built character and self-confidence. I'd had a lot of independence as a kid, and allowing him to have some, even for this moment, reminded us of how important this was. It also allowed him to start creating a healthy separation from us.

Living in other countries with different norms and values gave teachable moments everywhere that could build character and self-belief everywhere. We vowed to take advantage of every opportunity, although things didn't always go as smoothly as they had in Munich.

After spending five weeks in Germany and watching German parenting at the parks, playgrounds, shops, amusement parks, and beer gardens, we decided to let our kids have more autonomy. The first week we came back, we let Daniel go out with the bike on our street. We live in a thirty-house development with a street with a cul-de-sac. The cars going in and out are mainly from the neighborhood; people know there are kids around, and drive slowly. Daniel was so excited to bike without me being there, just like the kids in Germany.

Ten minutes into him being on the street, the doorbell ran. It was a neighbor, informing me that my son was alone in the street. I reassured her that I was aware of this.

"This is illegal in our state," she said. "I wouldn't be surprised if someone reports you to Child Services."

The shock of her words put my body into freeze. My legs in particular went numb, but since we'd just returned from travel, my brain was somehow still on high alert. I took a deep breath.

"It's very nice that you're concerned for Daniel," I told her. "And to be honest, I didn't think it was illegal for my son to bike outside our house by himself. I'll check on that. But if Child Services comes and has a problem with us, I'll know it was you who sent them."

"I would never do that," she said, quickly, backing away, her eyes wide.

The conversation is still so vivid in my memory that it still gives me goosebumps.

Afterwards, we read up about local regulations and our parents' rights. As foreigners, we sometimes know our rights better than the locals, but that's okay. I prefer to be informed than to live in limbo.

*"The best education you will ever get is traveling. Nothing teaches you more than exploring the world and accumulating experiences."*

*Mark Paterson*

***

A year later, after walking across half of Paris, we waited, exhausted, for a bus to get home. When it arrived, the people in front of us got on board, and Danny and Bella followed. Just as Nasko was about to get on, the bus driver closed the door and the bus started moving. My heart stopped. My voice disappeared.

Thankfully, the kids' voices didn't. They started to scream, "MOM! DAD!" The other bus passengers joined in, and the bus driver stopped so we could jump on. I had never been happier to hug my kids. They spoke over each other, crying.

"Why did he leave you at the bus stop?" "That was so scary!"

We had a long conversation that night about what to do if that were to happen again, or if they were ever kidnapped. Our kids didn't have cell phones at that time, so we agreed on a protocol:

1. They had done the right thing to scream.

2. If that happened again, they were to get off at the next stop and wait for us there.

3. We should always hold hands. If someone were to pull them from us, they should start screaming as loudly as they could.

4.  They had to pay attention to their surroundings and the people around them.

5.  They had to memorize our cell phone numbers. (I had already started writing my number on the inside of their wrists and covering it with liquid bandage.)

Back in school in the fall of that year, there were some incidents of an adult wandering suspiciously around the school while the kids were at recess. I shared with another mom that I had talked to Bella and Danny about kidnapping. She asked, "Aren't they too young for that?"

I told her about our experience in Paris.

The world will not wait for kids to grow up and be old enough to learn about it.

A few years after that, riding the bus home from school, Danny's bus driver had to reroute due to an accident.

Unfamiliar with the area, the driver turned to her young passengers. "Does anyone know an alternative route to the main road?" she called out.

The students were in grades six, seven, and eight. Nobody had a clue.

Daniel, then in grade six (twelve years old), stepped forward and assured the bus driver that he could guide her. She was skeptical, but agreed to follow his instructions. They were spot on, and everyone got home on time. As Daniel got off the bus at our home, the children erupted in cheers.

We never intentionally showed him different routes around the neighborhood, but we had invested time teaching our children the importance of paying attention to their surroundings. Once they grasped the concept, they applied it naturally. This incident taught us a lesson I had partly learned decades ago from my own parents: the importance of being patient with our kids and trusting their development—and also, of simply spending time with them. Through our guidance and our unwavering belief in our kids, we can empower them with skills that they'll use throughout their lives.

*"So, our job as parents is not to make a particular kind of child.
Instead, our job is to provide a protected space of love, safety, and stability in which children of many unpredictable kinds can flourish."*

*- Alison Gopnik*

# CHAPTER 28

# Societal Trap

One expectation I still hadn't managed to avoid was going overboard in getting my kids involved in "activities".

Like many parents, I fell into the collective fear that if we did not jam our children' s lives with every lesson, sport, and cultural activity in existence, they might somehow "fall behind". This idea that you must be a perfect parent, and that if you aren't, everyone will point at you and comment on how incompetent you are, is not just "big" in America. It's another relic of communism.

No wonder there's such collective burnout!

By the time the kids were both in elementary school, my afternoons felt like I was going into a boxing match. I'd prepare snacks and dinner, then navigate traffic while trying to listen to them share as much as they could about their school days. I hated being late–it made me feel small and uncommitted (another communist leftover: we were simply not allowed to be late to school), so I'd rush to their violin or piano lessons, then they'd have dinner in the car while I tried to listen to them talk about whatever they'd just learned while we raced to ice skating, or track and field, or gymnastics. Then a quick shower, and off to bed.

By the time they got to the second activity of the night, the kids were usually cranky and mad at each other, and at me. Bella had already fallen asleep in the car by the time we got home most evenings, and waking her only worsened her mood.

"When am I going to see them?" Nasko asked, one night. "They're always so tired when you get them home."

"I'm tired, too," I said, collapsing on the couch. I took a deep breath. "I don't want to do this anymore."

That night, the two of us realized that, in our attempt to sacrifice ourselves for the kids, we were all losing our connections with each other. We'd become caught in the societal traps of competing with other parents about whose child did more activities. Our kids didn't have any free time to play, never mind spending time with us or having family dinners, a ritual I especially cherished from the time that it was taken away from me and my own parents. There was no space to show our kids that they mattered; that they belonged. And they hadn't even reached high school yet. They were growing up in a world that is focused on doing. And we had lost our sense of the present moment, convinced that the next thing would hold more significance than the current moment we're experiencing.

The next day, we spoke with them.

"Guys, what would you think if we dropped some of the activities so you can have more free time?"

Danny perked up immediately. "Really? Which one?"

"If you could keep one, which one would it be?

"I like piano lessons; they make me relaxed."

"Okay, so piano stays for you. Bella, which one would you pick?"

"Violin," Bella said, without hesitation.

"Can we drop the rest?" I asked.

"I like ice skating too," Danny interjected, "but maybe we can go together, as a family?"

They were thrilled. They told everyone at school that they were going to have free time to play.

Of course, there were disapproving faces when other parents asked what my kids were up to after school.

I responded, "I let them be kids."

But if I'm honest, I did it for myself first and for the

kids second. As parents, we're "supposed to" forsake our own lives to provide for our kids. We're expected to live in a way that is always buzzing with activities, and to always be in control: pushing, optimizing, and achieving. Kids are supposed to get high marks and fit in with the right people. And parents, despite themselves, can become obsessed with our kids reaching their goals, because it supposedly equals the promise of a happy future. We believe it will give them opportunities we didn't have. Then we wonder why our kids have problems concentrating.

Once we stopped all the activities, the transformation was astounding. Both kids quickly became happier and more relaxed. They relished their free time after school, playing in the backyard, riding their bikes, or simply doing nothing. Instead of me lecturing and trying to motivate them in the car for the next activity, we granted them the freedom to live in the present was worth more than what they might miss out on learning, doing or "achieving". And we started having family dinners again, which had been such a cornerstone of my childhood, and which felt like such a huge loss during that after-school-activity-driven period.
Those times we spent together are some of my most precious memories.

*"The most dangerous phrase in language is:*

*"We've always done it this way"*

*- Grace Hopper*

# CHAPTER 29

# Price

Nasko and I decided to celebrate our tenth wedding anniversary with a trip to Rangali Island in the Maldives. I don't use the term "dream vacation" lightly, but it was.

I couldn't in the farthest reaches of my imagination have pictured water that blue and sand that white. Nasko went diving almost every day. I tried every massage and spa treatment they had. The resort staff were so accommodating. You couldn't find a reason to complain if you tried.

One day, soaking in the jacuzzi in our overwater bungalow, I realized that my heart had been clenched for the whole time, waiting for some unknown bad thing to come. I said, "This is too perfect."

I remembered a story from when I was young, back when my parents owned their stores in Bulgaria, and my brothers and I went in for a visit. One of the employees gave us each a wafer cookie. We were so excited, until my dad handed us some money to give to her.

"This is your store," I said, confused. "Why do you have to pay?"

"Because at the end of the day, when they close the register, they will be short of money."

My father was obsessed with the idea that nothing in life was free. He truly believed that there was a price for everything, including happiness—and not just a financial price. Happiness would cost you emotionally, down the line. I never questioned this belief.

On that holiday, I started to wonder: *what price will I have to pay for this happiness?*

After a few days on Rangali, we flew to Dubai, and then traveled to Abu Dhabi. There, Nasko lived one of his childhood dreams of driving an F3 car on the Yas Marina circuit. I'll never forget watching him beam as he put on the race suit and climbed into the car. After he drove the laps, when he got out and took off his helmet, the look on his face said it all: he was the happiest kid on the block.

On our way back to Dubai, I called my mom to wish her a happy birthday. She tried to play it cool, but something in her voice tipped me off.

"What's wrong?" I demanded. "Tell me."

She took a deep breath. "Your father is in the hospital.

It doesn't look good."

We were about to fly out of Dubai. As I processed this news, I knew that instead of flying back to Seattle, I could go directly to Bulgaria. I called my brothers, who had always been straightforward about the situation with my dad. They told me that things were really going downhill this time. Dad's liver was working only 20%. They were waiting for the doctors to give them the full story about how serious the situation was, but our flight was fast approaching. With no answers, they suggested I go back to Seattle.

After the fifteen-hour flight, I landed to find a message that I should fly to Bulgaria as soon as I could.

"This is it," I thought. "I had a beautiful experience, and now I will pay for it by losing my dad."

Nasko and I spent a few hours with the kids, explaining why I needed to leave again, and then I got on another flight. As soon as I boarded, time slowed. The weight of my thoughts seemed to be pushing against the forward motion of the plane.

Why now?

Why couldn't I just be happy without there being a cost?

I arrived in Bulgaria to find my father extremely

weak, but in much better shape than expected. The doctors had performed a miracle. They released him a week later, only to then inform us that he had only twenty-four to forty-eight hours to live.

My parents have always been such positive people. And home is a healing space, much more so than the hospital. We decided to wait and see. My dad was much better the next day. By afternoon he was talking, and even trying to walk. Two days later, he continued to improve. I decided to fly back home to my kids and Nasko.

My parents immediately changed their diet. They started reading and trying everything that made sense to them, with the only goal being to improve my father's health. His inflammation levels lowered, and his energy increased. But as time passed, he seemed to forget how scary his situation had been, and went back to his old way of life. The inflammation came back, he started retaining water, his energy levels dropped, and he started drinking again.

The next year, when I visited them, I noticed something was off. There was a certain carelessness about my dad. He'd spent hours sitting on the couch, staring at National Geographic TV, lost in his own world. We could come and go and he would not be bothered. And he was drinking every day.

Of course it reminded me of how he'd been after the banks collapsed, but I dismissed it. It's not an excuse, but

I was busy with my young kids, and decided that adults should know better, and that they were responsible for their own struggles.

"Dad is stronger than that," I'd thought.

But it continued. And even though someone on the outside might not pick up on it, we all felt it–even the kids. On our next visit, two years later, as we were about to return to the States, Bella began to cry.

"Can you promise that we will see them all again next time?" she sobbed.

It's mind-blowing how a 9-year-old can assess a situation.

I could see where things were probably headed. I said, "I can't promise you that they will all be here. I would be lying if I did. But we are here now, and we are with them; we have to cherish these moments."

The mind wants to keep us safe. It wants to keep us in the comfort zone with what's familiar; to protect us from danger. But my dad didn't have the ability to see that, and more to the point, he wasn't aware that there was anything wrong with what he was doing. Most people drink in Bulgaria, so in a way, it was "normal". I certainly never paid attention to it. And if we believe something is normal, we don't question it. It wasn't until I discovered RTT that I learned to question cultural norms.

My father continued to drink on and off. He began to worsen rapidly in November of 2019. He stopped drinking again, but by that point there was so much toxicity in his blood, his liver couldn't function. It was like he was in a coma–he was completely non-responsive. And once again, the doctors did their magic and saved him. December was another tough month, with more trips to the hospital and yet another magical save. Looking back, that would probably have been the time for me to visit him one last time, but I was in so much denial of what was happening. Then the kids started the ski season, and with so many happy days in the mountains, I just believed the magic would continue to work. That he would recover. That he would change.

But people don't change, especially when they are 60 years old and very sick–and even more so in Bulgaria, where there is a belief that when you get old, it's normal to be sick, and not to care, or really challenge things. To just sit and wait to die.

It really pisses me off.

The nineteenth century physician Henry Maudsley believed that unprocessed emotions, especially grief, can manifest as physical symptoms in the body. He said, "the sorrow that has no vent in tears may make other organs weep". (Bessel Van Kolk later addressed this same topic in his book *The Body Keeps the Score*, as did Gabor Mate in *When the Body Says No*.) The theory holds that stress weakens the heart, anger and worry weaken the liver, grief weakens the lungs, fear weakens the kidneys. Our entire body speaks and we are responsible to learn the language in order to understand it.

And addiction, as I later learned, is a progressive disease. If we have a big enough distraction, like Herbalife or the first health scare was for my dad, it can temporarily be stopped... but it always comes back. And, even with those "stops", it gets worse with time.

I did not yet know the truth about my father: that in his body, held the kind of trauma that no one could have processed without support.

But I believe he came to the point where he just gave up.

And when the mind gives up, the body gives up, too.

*"Never be a prisoner of
your past.
It was just a lesson, not a
life sentence."*

*- unknown*

# CHAPTER 30

# Awakening

When I was born, in my culture, most fathers wanted their first child to be a boy.

It was, of course, before doctors could know the sex of a baby.

*And* it was a time when no one was allowed in a birth hospital at that time other than the mother.

So when I came into the world, the nurse turned worriedly to my mom and said, "How are we going to tell your husband it's a girl?"

"Just call him," my mom said. "He'll be the happiest man on earth."

For all his imperfections, he was my hero. And when he died that day in February 2020, I felt pain that I still have no words to describe. The closest thing I can come to is, in fact, childbirth–first the excruciation, then the numbness, again and again. The repeated "contractions" of realizing that not only was he not next to me, but he never would be again. Reminiscing about him would bring a temporary pause in the suffering. The kids would ask how I was, and I would cry. Then something positive would happen, and the pain would ease, just for a few minutes. Up, down, again and again.

And then, a few weeks after he died, I had my experience that day on the mountain.

When the weight I'd never realized I'd been carrying lifted off me.

Nasko was skiing behind me, so he saw me stop.

"What happened?" he asked, as he caught up with me. "Are you okay?"

"I don't know," I said, breathless, "but I feel fantastic. It feels like something heavy that wasn't mine has just been taken from me. Like some kind of judgement."

I gasped.

"Do you think it was my dad's judgment of me?"

Nasko said, truthfully, that he didn't know. He stayed with me as we skied down, and for the rest of the day, I felt more and more energy pouring into me, like a battery being recharged.

This mysterious feeling continued in the days that followed. Even my breathing felt different. I decided that no matter what, I would wake up happy every day. Of course some days would be more difficult than others, but they were all here to teach me something. And even if I didn't see what that was right away, I would be ready for it.

***

I became obsessed with understanding what I'd experienced that day, and with finding out why my father had died.

Of course, you might be thinking, "He died of severe liver damage from drinking too much."

And you would be right. But something inside me—a persistent, undeniable feeling—kept insisting that there was more to the story. That there was something crucial I was missing; something important that no one was saying. The feeling jolted me awake in the pitch-black middle of the night, haunting me, refusing to let me rest until I found the answers.

By spring of that year, the entire world had stopped. We were in full pandemic lockdown, all trapped inside our homes, grasping for some sense of normalcy. As was the case for many, our kids' education system began to come apart at the seams. Everyone was trying to figure out technology none of us had relied on before, with exhausted teachers begging kids to turn on their cameras while over-whelmed parents attempted to join work meetings in the background. Everything felt broken.

Nasko and I took a look at this disaster and decided we would take control of what we could. Although we continued to keep up with the news, we stopped watching it on television, putting a boundary up against fear blasting out of a screen. I enrolled in courses to get state-certified in homeschooling so I could properly help the kids navigate their crumbling education. I also found an online accelerator program organized by other parents who wanted to save their kids' education.

In this accelerator program, people presented topics that went beyond our kids' education. I was astonished by every new discovery. We learned about memory and brain foods, mindful technology... the science of exercise and gut microbiomes... biohacking... childhood trauma... sleep types and more. I looked forward to each session.

Of all the topics we covered, my favourite was about how the way we've been parented affects who we become as adults. I began reading and watching everything I could get my hands on about generational cycles, trying to catch up on a universe I had never knew existed. I was starting to see how many of us carry the exact same understandings as our parents did, and how, without realizing it, we repeat the same beliefs and behaviours as they did—especially in cultures like mine, which carry such a stigma around seeking help for mental health. I became determined to know how my "perfect" childhood had affected my adulthood, and how it was affecting my kids. The more I learned, the hungrier I became to peel back the layers.

One theme we discussed was how important it is to listen to your kids when they want to talk to you. Sounds obvious, right? But looking back, I saw how many times I'd brushed Bella and Danny away when I was working, cooking, or doing something "important". I learned that when we do this, our children internalize a message: *I am not important. My parent's work is more important than me.* We rarely stop to think about what our kids feel when we reject them. The kids were ten and twelve years old by then, and it had certainly never occurred to me.

That night, when we sat down for dinner, I said, "Kids, I want to apologize."

They looked stunned.

"For the times I wasn't the parent you wanted me to be," I continued. "For the times when you needed me and I was preoccupied with work, cooking, or something else. For the times when I had high expectations that caused you frustration. And for the times I used my authority to insist on you doing what I want, without even considering what you wanted."

They were still shocked, but also, I could see that they understood. I explained that parents make mistakes, too.

We talked about how mistakes make us feel, and how to reflect on and learn from them. I think that was the first moment they saw me as a human, rather than a mom.

"I promise I will prioritize you over work," I told them. "I will listen to you. I will consider all your opinions. I will review my expectations of you, and make them more realistic. We are in this together." I paused. "But sometimes, I might need reminding. From you."

"We can do that," they said, enthusiastically. They sounded… different. Empowered.

"But will you promise not to be mad at us when we do?" Daniel asked, catching my gaze.

"Absolutely. From here on in, we will be partners."

"Like you and Dad are partners?" Bella asked.

"To some degree, yes."

The air in the room changed. I felt closer to them, like we were all on the same team. To this day, when one of us is trying to do it "all", we say to each other, "Remember, we're all in this together."

I continued to learn by trial and error. I still had to retrain myself from being "too busy" for the kids, and to make myself stop, reflect, and learn. I began reading more about neuroscience and neuroplasticity, cognitive behavior, and Neuro-Linguistic Programming.

That's when I discovered Rapid Transformational Therapy.

The concept of RTT–discovering the power of the human mind–resonated with me immediately. When I heard that Marissa Peer, the founder, was offering a free 30-minute recorded visualization, I was curious, but on high alert. With my upbringing, I still questioned everything and wanted to make sure this wasn't a situation where I'd be taken advantage of.

The visualization was about money. I asked Nasko to join me. As it began, we entered into the meditative state of hypnosis, and I felt my body relax. My conscious mind drifted away, and to my surprise, I was guided straight to a scene from my childhood right after communism collapsed in Bulgaria: those completely empty shelves at our local store. The coupon system to buy bread. No food, no clothes, no gas.

I wasn't reliving that moment–I was simply there, reviewing it, as if watching a movie on a screen.

The picture was astonishingly clear. The feeling flooded my body, just like it did back then: that money was cold, and had no value. That money was never enough. The experience was so real, but I was looking at it with my adult eyes, and understanding it with my present-day mind. I could see how I was still stuck here. How even though I had so much in my life, I was still acting from a place of being in this belief.

The recording took us through a process of letting go of our belief about money, and, for me, seeing what I was actually living in today. After the practice ended, I turned to Nasko.

"That was amazing," he said, his eyes shining. "I was taken straight back to my childhood, after the collapse."

This belief I had carried for so long, that money was temporary and that it could be here today and gone tomorrow, began to fade. Over the following months, Nasko and I began to realize that we'd been pursuing a specific figure or goal, and that this had become a never-ending race, with the finish line always moving further and further away. No amount of money was ever going to make us happy if we lived with mistaken beliefs around it.

This weight lifted from our shoulders, and in its place, something ignited: a desire to understand how money worked, and to see how we could save it in a way that would secure our future. This concept of planning—of providing ourselves with years of peace and comfort after retirement—was new to me, but I welcomed it. In fact, I read and studied as much as I could, and asked Nasko to teach me everything he'd learned.

My goals started to shift. I wanted to enjoy my family more: to be present for dinner conversations, to hear my kids' laughter, to spend time with Nasko without my mind being somewhere else. I wanted to continue traveling, to meet fascinating new people whose stories would change me, to immerse myself fully in rich, vibrant cultures so different from my own. I didn't want to wait for some vague, mythical "someday", or retirement, or an empty nest—some magical future moment when life would finally slow down—to finally start living intentionally and joyfully. I wanted to live right now, while I still had time, while my kids were still young, while I still could. But I also wanted to be responsible, thoughtful, and mindful of our future security.

Life was too short and too precious to keep postponing.

Nasko and I both loved that Marisa's method was able to get to deep core beliefs so quickly, and how we were able to overcome the strong resistance of our conscious minds and change our fundamental beliefs using the power of hypnosis. I saw how long I'd been stumbling through life with tunnel vision, oblivious to the countless paths that had stretched before me. How in my cluelessness, I'd unknowingly made choices that had forever altered the course of my life (although I think sometimes knowing less and doing your best gives us the most important life lessons).

What stories had my dad carried in his mind? I wondered. What beliefs had navigated his life? Which ones did I inherit from him? I'd been haunted that there was more than just a medical explanation for his passing. Now, I'd found a practice that could help me explore that: to learn about the connection between body and mind, to the point that they can affect when our life ends.

There were so many modalities and options available, but I was drawn to RTT because it delivered such fast results. Working the subconscious mind goes directly to the root causes of our issues, giving clients results in between one and three sessions—a much quicker process than traditional talk therapy, which has an average results time of fifteen to twenty sessions. To me, RTT felt like an emergency room for healing limiting beliefs, emotional patterns, and behaviour that are all interconnected.

I devoured everything I could find about the RTT training program. I read obsessively, researched compulsively, and analyzed every detail. I started the application process, my heart pounding with excitement and fear. Every cell in my body wanted this. I could feel it physically: it felt right, important, and meant-to-be. While I'd been working on my flower business, I had been taking online psychology classes as well. This opportunity to train in RTT felt like an unrecognized desire coming straight from my heart.

But my sabotaging monkey mind kept provoking me.

*Can you do it? Is this what you really want? It seems so complicated!*

When my application was finished, my finger hovered over the "submit" button for a full minute before I finally hit "apply".

*"It is not what you are that holds you back. It is what you think you are not.*
*You are always one decision away from totally different life."*

*- Mel Robbins*

# CHAPTER 31

# New Beginning

I was interviewed five separate times for the RTT training program over the following few weeks, sometimes for an hour and a half at a time. The interviewers would present me with complex potential client situations around trauma, addiction, deep-seated fears, and challenge me without mercy.

"How would you handle this specific case?"

"What therapeutic approach would you take?"

"Walk us through your entire thought process."

I enjoyed the interview process without taking it too seriously. Even though I was convinced I was failing terribly, I felt even more excited after each interview.

After what felt like an eternity, I got the call.

"We've found you to be an excellent match for our program," the man said from the other end of the phone.

Time stopped.

I couldn't breathe. I couldn't process what I was hearing. I stood in my kitchen, a loud rushing sound in my ears as he talked enthusiastically about next steps and start dates.

Against every doubt, every fear, every limiting belief... I'd done it.

And then, out of my clenched mouth, came the sound of my voice.

"I'm not interested," I said, and hung up.

I'd nailed the enrollment. Doing anything more felt too scary. Truthfully, I didn't feel like I could spend such a large amount of money on something just for me. Nasko was making more money than I was, and although he never once brought it up, I was stuck in the idea that I wasn't doing enough or providing enough. It was another one of my firmly held money beliefs, instilled when my parents lost all of theirs.

I didn't want to be a burden.

Nasko, of course, called me out on this. He reminded me of how much I loved the online psychology class. He told me it was time to do something for myself. He even spoke to my money fears.

"You can even finance it through your business," he said.

So I emailed them back and enrolled.

I'm grateful to Nasko for so many reasons, but that day was one of the biggest ones: that he saw possibility in me, and encouraged me to follow my heart. After studying interior design and architecture for my dad, and public administration and law for my mom, I studied human behaviour and generational cycles for me.

But still, at Christmas of that year, at least with regards to generational cycles, I hit my rock bottom.

***"Healthy habits are
learned in the same way
as unhealthy ones - try
practice."***

*- Wayne Dyer*

# CHAPTER 32

# Rock Bottom

Every Christmas, we have a family tradition. We all head out to a local farm to pick a tree. We bring it home, put on some festive music, and make hot cocoa. Then we bring out the boxes of ornaments, and decorate the tree together. It's one of my absolute favorite times of the year. And that year, the kids really wanted to do the tree themselves.

After they had gone to bed, I took in what they'd done. It was nice, of course, but the ornaments were all crammed together at the front, which was as far as they could reach. I started taking each one down, thinking that I would spread them out around the tree to make it perfect.

Nasko was lying comfortably on the couch, watching TV. At a certain point, he looked up, and hit pause on the remote control.

"What are you doing?" he asked.

I explained my mission, indicating how the shoved-together decorations at the front of the tree were a problem and how they were not aesthetically pleasing.

"What do you think the kids are going to think tomorrow?"

My hand, holding an ornament, hovered in mid-air. It hadn't once occurred to me what my redecorating would spell out to the kids: that they didn't do a good enough job. That I wasn't happy with their work.

I was still obsessed with control.

I've learned that the desire to control our outer world is usually triggered by the need to keep things as structured and predictable as possible, because that's the only way we feel safe. For me, safety and certainty had collapsed along with communism. There had been so much uncertainty since then that I hadn't understood, but it had imprinted on me. (Not to mention genetic patterns from the uncertainty in my father's childhood, but I knew nothing about that yet.) I was in a never-ending race of perfection, which would come at the cost of my kids' self-esteem, never mind my own mental health.

Our culture conditions us to believe that control will make us happy. But if you think about the best moments in your life, I'll bet you they're the moments when you gave up control and just enjoyed what was happening.

That night, I pulled out my phone, found the photo the kids had taken of their work earlier that evening, and hung every ornament back where they had originally placed it.

And as soon as I could, I called an RTT therapist and scheduled a session.

In this session, I went back to the multiple times my dad had told me:

"You can take care of yourself."

"You can change a light bulb by yourself."

"You can make lunch for yourself."

He'd been empowering me to believe in myself, teaching me different skills in order to be self-sufficient. But my young self had taken it to the next level: "I have to do it myself in order to be perfect."

I'd known where my problem was coming from, but it had been too hard for my logical mind to override the feelings attached to it. Now, I had the understanding on a subconscious level. I saw how despite how hard Nasko and I had worked to come to a place where we shared the housework, I was again doing all the cleaning, cooking, and taking care of the house, as if I were the only one living here who could do any of this. I was doing all the shopping alone. I loaded and unloaded the groceries from the car by myself. I did all the yardwork. I even organized every date night and every anniversary Nasko and I ever celebrated, and every other party and celebration, no matter how small or big. Yes, I always consulted with Nasko, but that's where it stopped, even though he wanted to help. I even bought myself flowers.

Which is fine, except then I would say to Nasko, "Thanks for buying me flowers today, they are beautiful!"

I didn't realize how I was taking away his pleasure of giving me something.

And all the while, I was still working, building my small business DidiArtCorner.

"Stay-at-home Mom" didn't produce anything tangible that could be put on a spreadsheet, so in American culture, it didn't count.

The kids were eight and ten years old by then. They could easily have participated in helping around the house, but it didn't occur to me to ask. I had the time to do it, and I felt guilty for having that time, and when I got laid off and had even more time, I felt even more guilty.

But after that RTT session, I said, "I'm no longer available to do all of this."

We started to cook together. The kids took turns setting the table and loading the dishwasher. Nasko and

Danny took over most of the yard work, and we planned the week and the weekends together, setting up a shared calendar where everyone included their own events. This didn't happen overnight–it took time. But I no longer carried the guilt that was pushing me so hard to do it all alone, and pushing them out of the picture. I wasn't "leading" anymore. We became a team.

I also let Nasko organize a day for the two of us. He bought me flowers and took us for a massage, then for dinner.

"Where are we going?" I kept asking him, or, "Shouldn't we park here?"

Finally, he said, "I know where to park. Let go."

The day turned out to be magical, and by allowing him to take charge, I felt lighter. From then on, I started embracing imperfection: allowing others to have control, to lead, to make choices without me trying to get in the way. It was taking time, but letting go, and not doing everything alone, was starting to feel good.

> **"The secret of change is to focus all of your energy not on fighting the old, but on building the new."**
>
> *- Dan Millman*

# CHAPTER 33

# Rediscovering Dad

After my dad passed away, my mom's first reaction was relief.

Of course she missed him. They had been life partners for 40 years, doing everything together until he died. But at first, after he passed, she just felt calm. She'd been his primary caregiver for so long, and it had taken its toll on her, especially over the past year. She would call me and share how strange it felt to come home from work and actually have time for herself. She and my grandma would sit and chat, sharing memories about my dad. She remembered my father with peace and joy, as if the grief didn't exist.

And she slept. A lot.

Meanwhile, she was following my pursuit of becoming an RTT practitioner with interest. She understood how much it meant to me, and was fascinated with how many unprocessed feelings from childhood I was carrying.

One day, on a video call, I asked her what she knew about my dad's childhood.

"Not much," she admitted. "I know it was rough, but he never talked about it."

"Was he abused? Physically and verbally, by his parents?"

She let out a sharp breath. "How did you know that? We've never talked about this. He never told anyone."

"He told me," I said.

She was stunned.

I explained to my mom that my dad hadn't literally told me what had happened; that I'd learned it in hypnosis. In the RTT process, there's a tool that allows the client to ask questions about their past and get answers, even if the people involved are no longer alive. I'd chosen to ask Dad.

"Something significant happened to Dad when he was fifteen years old," I told her. "Do you know what it was?"

She went silent for what it felt like an eternity. Finally, she said, "He was heavily abused, physically and mentally, by both his parents, but mainly by his mom."

Now it was my turn to gasp.

"He was 15 when they got divorced," she went on. "Neither of them was interested in caring for him, so they kicked him out of the house. Luckily, he had very kind neighbors who took care of him, and he stayed in school until he began his mandatory military service."

I was almost speechless. This had been a significant part of my dad's life. Did I even know who he was?

"Why didn't you guys tell me–tell us–any of this?"

"He almost never talked about it, even with me. This is all I know."

"You didn't ask him?"

"I did, but he always found a way to ignore it. I saw how painful it was for him and decided to let him have it his way. "

I shook my head. "I feel like I'm just getting to know him, even though he just died," I told her.

My mom nodded. "I feel the same way."

My dad's parents had passed away by then, but his elder brother was still alive. He'd been my favourite uncle while I was growing up, and was married to my favourite aunt. They lived on the other side of Bulgaria and once my parents had stopped traveling, we'd all lost touch.

Mom reached out to my uncle, who confirmed that all of the stories I had "received" from my dad in the hypnotherapy session were true. The neglect, the abuse, all of it.

I'm sure my father's parents had their reasons for how they behaved. It's not an excuse, but their own struggles made them the parents they had become. But to me, this was a deeper understanding of generational cycles, and how hard my dad had tried to build a new route and a different life, absent of any verbal or physical abuse.

And he'd done it, successfully, for us.

But he'd never know what to do with his own unprocessed trauma and stuck feelings. He hadn't known that "the body keeps the score"; that he could have processed the feelings and emotions that he kept stuck in his body, not knowing what to do with it, and freed himself from the unbearable pain of his childhood. He did what he thought was helpful: he never talked about it, and he parented the opposite way of how his parents had raised him.

My gut had always told me there was something more than medical behind the decline in health that led to my father's death. You can't let go of something if you don't understand it, and now I was gaining that exact understanding: Dad didn't have any safety, care, or support when he was a child. He had done everything in his power to outrun his demons, but they had caught up with him. His feelings had slowly eaten him alive.

In Japan, there is an ancient art called Kintsugi[8]. When a piece of pottery breaks, instead of throwing away the pieces, they glue them back rootogether with gold that highlights all the cracks. The piece's flaws then make it more beautiful than before. Kintsugi teaches us that our scars are not signs of weakness, but symbols of strength and survival. Like those golden seams, they tell a story of healing, resilience, and transformation. Our imperfections don't make us less. They make us who we are. Our cracks are where the light gets in.

Finally, my father became human to me. He will forever be my superhero, but now I know that this superhero had many struggles and flaws. But I put his story back together with golden glue and embraced all those cracks, because imperfection is beautiful.

---

[8] See Notes -P295

**"Death is the enemy of the dead;
grief is the enemy of the living."**

*- William Shakespeare*

# CHAPTER 34

# Grief

One day, a few months after my dad died, my mom called me at an unusual time, given our time difference. She was hyperventilating so hard I could barely understand her.

"He is gone, my home is empty, my heart is empty, my head is pulsing," she sobbed. "I can't find a place for myself. I don't know what to do."

The reality was finally hitting her. This is a normal stage of the grieving process, but she had no idea what to do with it. I'd suspected this would happen sooner or later, and had taken extra time to work with grief in my training, including all its stages and how to process it, so I could be there for her when it happened.

First, I helped her calm down—to sit with her feelings and "become a detective", exploring each one, where she felt it in her body, what it felt like.

"I've never taken the time to notice my feelings like this," she said.

"I know," I reassured her. "A lot of people say the same thing."

"I feel so much better just sharing with you about them. I can breathe now. I can feel my heart. Some kind of calmness is settling over me."

I could tell she was fascinated. I stayed with her for a long time and made sure she was okay, then let her get a good night's rest.

The next day, I asked her how she was doing.

"It was the first time in a long time I actually slept! I feel so recharged today, like a new person. But I see myself in a different way."

"What do you mean?"

"I'm me, but calmer. Wiser, in a way. The way you helped me process those feelings felt so freeing."

I acknowledged that this was the whole idea—to release feelings—but how we often don't know what to do with them, so we keep them in.

"Gosh," she said. "I can't imagine how much your dad carried with him."

In a way, it was like she, too, had finally allowed my dad's spirit to fly away.

She went on, "Last night–I had a session with you, didn't I?"

"Kind of," I said. "I used some of the tools to help you process all that you had at that time, but it wasn't a deep session."

"Do you think I'm ready for a deep session?"

I explained that she might need a few more days to process before a real RTT session. She felt so good, but she sensed that she had more to let go of. I explained that if we did a real session, we'd be going very deep and that she had to be honest with me, "almost like stripping naked".

"Can you do that with me?" I asked.

"I don't have anything to hide," she said. "And you'll learn about my childhood, too, which will help you."

A week later, my mom had her first RTT session with me. I set firm boundaries, reminding her that in this process, she would be talking to a therapist, not her daughter. In the session, she shared a lot about her father physically abusing her mom, which she had shared about with me before. But her real helplessness came up, which was about not being able to protect her mom, as she was just a child at the time. That helplessness had prevented her from having more confidence and self-esteem as she got older.

"I just lost 20 kilos," she said, after we were done. "Those feelings were heavy. I can breathe more easily now."

We managed to keep the boundaries in place. When she called afterwards, for follow-up or with questions, she always said, "Hello there, I am looking for my therapist." When it was about something else, she'd say, "Hi, I am looking for my daughter."

We'd laugh, but this differentiation of our roles worked for both of us.

235

*"History is not destiny,
our past could be under-
stood,
but it doesn't dictate our
present and our future.
We don't have to run from
our past nor we have to be
insulted by."*

*-Tina Bryson*

# CHAPTER 35

# Shuttered

The pandemic restrictions were lifting. I had done as much online RTT training as I could, so I flew to LA for in-person training

I was so excited from the moment I boarded the plane, not just for the destination, but for the thrill of traveling again after so long. I had met so many of the people online who'd be at the course, I couldn't wait to connect with them in person: for their voices to become real; for their faces to no longer be just pixels on a screen. And of course, I was thrilled to be able immerse myself in this practice that had captured my heart.

We touched down and I felt a rush of energy as I stepped off the plane into the warm California air. The taxi ride was a blur of palm trees and sunshine. I met my room-mate Eunice in the hotel lobby, and within moments, it felt like we'd known each other for years. We rolled our suitcases toward the elevator, chatting like old friends. Early the next morning, we got coffee and walked through the quiet morning streets, a ritual that would become our routine for the duration of the training. There was something refreshing about those early hours, with the world just beginning to stir while we were already focused, ready for the day.

I immersed myself in the training, soaking up every word; every lesson. My heart had longed for this understanding. It made me feel so alive. Despite how packed they were, the days flew by.

One of the most memorable parts of the training was the live sessions, where someone would experience being an RTT client while the rest of us observed. At the beginning of these sessions, the trainers would always say, "If any of you get triggered from any of the live sessions, there are a lot of us—come see one of us for help."

"How can someone get triggered?" I wondered. "We've studied so many sessions already, some extremely difficult. I've seen it all!"

One day, a woman named Maggie volunteered to be the subject in a live session training. There were about 80 of us there, seated in a beautiful conference room filled with natural light from the floor-to-ceiling windows, our chairs positioned theater-style. In the front were two bar stool chairs with a bar table between them. RTT Founder

Marissa Pier sat on one side, and Maggie on the other.

Maggie shyly introduced herself and explained why she was here.

"I've tried everything else," she said. "This is my last hope. I have no reason to live."

Then she burst into tears.

The room became deathly quiet. Marissa sat patiently, without any change in her facial expression.

"I'm glad you're here," she said. "How would you like me to help you?"

For me, from that moment on, everyone else vanished. It was just me and Maggie.

"I was born in Communist China," Maggie began. "My parents emigrated to the US when they were in their twenties. I was left behind to stay with my grandparents."

Something began to move inside my chest. I thought about how my own great-grandparents had cared for me; how much love they'd given me.

"I came to the States when I was three years old, after my parents had been here for two years," Maggie went on. "On a trip to Disneyland, my dad was killed by a car while he was crossing the road."

My heart began beating faster.

Maggie kept talking. She spoke about her immigrant life, and all the loneliness it carried. About her struggle to thrive. About missing her parents, and a home with alcohol abuse. About unconditional love from one set of grandparents who were no longer there. It felt like a mirror that was slowly cracking.

My tears started flowing.

I stepped out of the room to get some air and try to calm myself. When I went back inside, I heard Maggie say,

"My other grandma saw me as stupid and incapable. When my caring and loving grandpa passed away, I was not able to go to the funeral."

The mirror broke.

I was suddenly crying so hard I couldn't breathe. What was happening to me? Why did I feel like my insides were spilling out? Yes, there were parallels, but I'd had a happy childhood. I was happy now! I had Nasko and my kids. I had a great life. Maggie only had her devastated, still-grieving mother, and the grandma back in China who had abused her.

I kept going outside the room, collecting myself, going back inside, listening for a few minutes, then having to leave again.

Maggie and Marissa got to the regression part of the session, where the subject visits three scenes from their past to discover the root cause[9] of the issue at hand. Then came the transformation, when they connect the past to their present life and all the old beliefs are resolved and dissolved. I went back inside the room for that part, but while Maggie transformed, I continued to bawl. I had never cried like this before, even when my father had died. (In fairness, I barely *had* cried before in my life. It was like I was making up for lost time.)

And even here, in this training, where we'd specifically been instructed to ask for help, I clung to my belief that I had to figure everything out by myself. Even though I could leave and come back in, I felt trapped, as if I were in a room with no exit. Finally, after the session ended, I asked one of the trainers if she'd sit with me and try to help me figure out what was going on.

"Where is it in your body?" she asked me. "How long has it been there? What's happening in your body now?"

Despite having coached my mom to feel her feelings, I barely ever paid attention to my own. I'd collected so many over my lifetime, it felt like there were too many to sort through. We went over them one by one: grief, resentment, control, the need to be seen for who I am, the need to be accepted, sadness, loneliness, being left out, not being good enough, being different... every one of them had been shut in, in an attempt to keep control.

By the time I finally stopped crying, I realized that the

---

[9] See Notes -p 295

conference room had emptied out ages ago. That kind trainer had stayed with me, focusing on me as if there were nowhere else on earth she'd rather be than helping me sort through the last 40 years of my life. She was so patient, so gentle. She modeled for me how to never rush a session. Some people just need more time than others.

But I still needed to talk. Luckily, Eunice was happy to hold space. We dimmed the lights in our room so it felt cosy and warm, and she listened without judgement as I shared more suppressed feelings, stories, and beliefs attached to them. The more we talked, the more the feelings lost their power. I could see them with curiosity until they melted away. I felt like I had unloaded the heaviest cargo imaginable which I had been holding onto with my whole life. It was as if I could finally see life clearly, and see the qualities I (and all of us) are born with: self-love, self-worth, self-confidence. I felt that transformed, like a newborn taking her first breath. I felt so excited for what awaited me in life. It felt like driving a car with a dirty window that was now, suddenly, completely clean.

Two days later, I called Nasko and said, "You're getting a new wife at the end of the week."

Still, part of me doubted the experience I'd just had. Was this some kind of midlife crisis? Where had all of these feelings been stored? How did this huge, black hailstorm come out of a clear blue sky? How did this upgrade happen so fast, why people stay stuck until the end of their lives, like my dad? I was trying to make sense of it all, for me and for my future clients.

And honestly, maybe it was a midlife crisis. It might have taken a bit longer if it hadn't been for that RTT experience, but it was going to happen either way. I believe that as humans, we are vessels for emotion, with only a limited capacity. Once we've had enough experiences and events that we haven't processed, they need to come out, which often occurs around midlife. When they don't come out, something has to give. That's what happened with my dad: the explosion went inwards, and he drank to keep it that way. I was lucky enough to crash, cry, and weep it all out.

**"Enough with the puppet
show we play for everyone.
It is time to live for ourselves."**

*-   Srimanju Katragadda*

***

I became a certified RTT therapist, and later, a clinical hypnotherapist and life coach. I went on to specialize in generational cycles and became a proud breaker of the ones that did not work for my kids and me. Life became so much easier when I let go of everything that was not in my control and focused on what was: myself.

But I wasn't there yet. I still had to face my biggest challenge yet. Like all good "trials", this one was set to tackle me when I least expected it: a few days after I returned home.

*"Once you surrender to living in your truth, in your light, and in your love, it shall set you free. When you are ready to be the change in your life, to break down the rules and walls that trap you, to make a new way out of no way, and breakthrough to your freedom, the universe shows up out of nowhere to help you do it."*

*- Zainab Salbi.*

# CHAPTER 36

# Surrender

It was supposed to be a regularly scheduled mammogram. I had it as soon as I arrived back in Seattle, and thought nothing of it. The clinic called me a few days after I had it and told me something I didn't understand, but which I took to mean that they had messed up the imaging and needed to do it again.

"Why are they taking pictures for a second time?" I asked the technician.

"We saw some calcifications," she told me. "We just wanted to make sure everything is okay."

A spike of fear shot through me, but I was surprised at how calm I felt overall. The tech explained that she wasn't allowed to tell me more, and that I should speak to my doctor.

They scheduled me for a biopsy a week later. I was

still managing to keep myself fairly steady, but the anxiety was starting to rise. I'd had bad experiences with dental anaesthesia, and wanted as few interferences in my body as possible. My plan to try to do this biopsy without anesthesia, relying solely on the techniques I'd studied in RTT about self-hypnosis, which research[10] had proven could minimize the body's cardiovascular response to pain.

When I told the doctor about my plans, he said, "We're doing a stereotactic core needle biopsy. It's a big deal. You need anesthesia. Plus, it will help you recover—and also, it will prove to your insurance that there are no complications."

For the record, my insurance would have covered the biopsy no matter if there was anaesthesia or not. But if I didn't get it, the clinic wouldn't be able to add it to my bill. The doctor refused to see past the money they would collect from my fear.

---

[10] See Notes -p 295

249

*"The moment you change
your perception;
is the moment you rewrite
the chemistry of your
body."*

*- Dr. Bruce Lipton*

***

A week after the biopsy, I got an email urgently advising me to set up a consultation with a surgeon, who would explain the results and tell me about my options. Every communication felt laced with more fear, as if it were all designed to make me feel like I only had minutes left to live.

Nasko came with me to the appointment. I needed him to think straight if I couldn't, and of course, I needed his strength.

The surgeon was a beautiful woman, slightly older than me. She jumped straight to the point, her voice breathless with urgency.

"You've been diagnosed with atypical ductal hyperplasia. The classifications that the biopsy we found statistically turn into cancer in five years or less, in 20% of cases."

"Statistically?" I repeated. "20%? In the next five years?"

These numbers didn't seem that high to me.

She rattled off a further avalanche of statistics, figures, and numbers. Each one landed like a heavy blow. Then, she launched into a list of treatment options, outlining each procedure as though it was to begin right then and there in her cold, sterile office.

Her words started to blur together. My body felt hollow, and like even if I tried to speak, no sound would come out.

"...radiation therapy and systemic therapy, which I will have to consult for details about with the oncologist..."

"Oncologist?" I blurted out. "Do I have cancer?"

She gave me the 20%, five-year statistic again.

"The last treatment option is a bilateral mastectomy," she concluded, and sat back in her seat.

I was speechless. How could this beautiful woman sit in front of me and casually suggest that I remove both my breasts?

Before I had the chance to speak, she leaned in again. "If it were me, I'd go with a double mastectomy."

She said it without feeling, as if we were making a business deal.

A sudden burst of energy flooded my body. I had nothing to lose. I thought, "I'll show you how I can fix this without a double mastectomy."

I looked her in the eye.

"Thank you for your opinion and the detailed consultation," I said. "I will give myself six months to heal."

She seemed shaken for a moment, and then rattled off the statistics again. More danger. More fear.

"I will take the risk," I said. "I will heal myself."

She gave me a look that suggested I was delusional. Then, like a salesperson who'd lost a sale, she huffily made me sign some paperwork stating that I'd been informed of my "diagnosis" and that I was refusing treatment at that moment.

We agreed that I would do a new mammogram in six months and go from there.

"Nothing will change," she said. "And you will have lost six months that might be critical for your condition."

I went home and read every piece of research and every study related to my case. I learned how to read mammogram images, and how to understand the medical terms used in the text that described them. I pored over mammograms that were similar to mine, and found one sentence in my own report that gave me great hope:

"No invasive carcinoma was identified."

I felt like I'd been medically bullied. Were they seeing dollar signs instead of a human being?

The first book I read during those weeks was *When the Body Says No* by Gabor Maté. The book explores the link between emotional stress and physical illness, including breast cancer. Maté suggests that chronic stress can contribute to the development of various diseases. He doesn't directly state that breast cancer is caused by not being able to say "no," but does argue that the inability to establish healthy boundaries and express emotions can be a significant contributing factor.

That stuck with me.

Maté clarifies that emotional stress can contribute to the disease's development by influencing various physiological processes, including the immune system and hormonal balance. Listening to the audio version of the book on my walk one morning, it dawned on me that I recognized myself in this description. I was still putting everyone else's needs before my own.

I thought, "A mother cares for a baby, feeding with breastmilk. Is that why it hit me in the breast? To remind me to stop?"

I jumped headfirst into prioritizing myself.

I had been mostly off sugar for a while, but now I removed it completely. I ate more vegetables to help my cells rejuvenate. Following the "Wim Hof" method, I took cold showers to reduce inflammation, fortify the immune system, balance the hormone levels, improve sleep quality, and increase my endorphins. I cleaned up my cosmetics, doing my best to avoid ingredients like sulfates, phthalates, parabens, and synthetic fragrances.

I did RTT sessions on myself every day. I would instruct my cells and body to function as nature intended, visualizing a healing vortex coming through my body that cleaned all the calcifications, then left through my feet and went into the ground. It was such a powerful exercise, I could actually sense it happening.

I kept asking myself, "Am I putting myself first?" Before cooking dinner, I'd sit in a short meditation to recharge my batteries. I taught the kids how to do the laundry and let them take over that chore completely. I scheduled grocery trips so that Nasko and I could go together. I made sure to wake up early and go for a morning walk, which I love—especially after a rainy night, when the air is so fresh and crisp. I started showing my kids that I didn't need to sacrifice myself for our family to function properly.

In my work today, I see how we play four roles in life: the brilliant, the sick, the rebel, and the carer. We adapt these roles when we're children in order to receive love, feel significant, and feel connected. Generally, in families, each person has a different role. The brilliant ones are people who are lauded for being academically or athletically successful as children. They become highly competitive people who can never stay away from work, and who are obsessed with being the absolute best at what they do. The sick start out as kids who didn't get much attention—but when they developed a chronic illness, they begin to matter. These people often grow up to be hypochondriacs. Rebels got attention as children only when they were difficult and caused problems. They often grow up to be addicts. And carers are valued because they look after everyone else, putting their own needs aside. (Interestingly, most therapists are carers.) I learned my carer role from my dad. He cared for a lot of people, but never took care of himself.

This was shocking to realize, but even more shocking was when I saw that Bella had taken on the carer role as well, but even more extreme. She had never allowed us to tie her shoes, or to help carry her luggage when we traveled. She never accepted us serving her water or food—if she wanted something, she got it herself. If she wanted cookies, she'd find the recipe and make them, instead of asking me to go to the store and buy them for her. They say the teacher succeeds when the students surpass them.

Six months later, I returned for another mammogram.

The surgeon had instructed me to see an oncologist afterwards. Seattle is one of the best places in the United States for breast cancer research, so I made sure to get an appointment with a doctor who was listed as the top cancer research oncologist for our area. I was excited to meet someone who had so much experience behind them.

He entered the room, introduced himself, and said, "So there are a number of treatment options we can work with. He went over a list, including a drug treatment and different levels of chemotherapy for breast cancer risk reduction.

Nasko and I listened patiently until he finished.

"That's fascinating," I said, "and I appreciate you explaining this to us in such detail. Fortunately, we don't need any of those.

His eyebrows shot up. He looked... well, angry.

"What do you mean, you don't need any of those?" He scanned my chart and read my initial diagnoses. "I see a diagnosis of atypical ductal hyperplasia. These are the treatments we do."

"I understand that, but that was six months ago. My current mammogram images are all clear. I don't have any calcifications."

"Let me see those images. Those things don't just disappear, you know."

"I made them disappear."

He opened his laptop and looked at the images.

He looked at me, then at Nasko.

He zoomed in to the images and zoomed out.

He looked at me again.

"There are no calcifications here," he said, quietly.

"Yes, I know. That's what I've been saying. I don't need chemo."

"How did that happen? What did you do?

"I changed my life, including my diet. I used to care for everyone but myself, so now I put myself first. I started breathwork and visualization. I did a lot of RTT and meditation."

"What's RTT?"

I explained. He looked at me like I was completely nuts, then waved me off. "Okay. Whatever."

He was one of the city's top cancer researchers, and he couldn't have cared less what I was telling him. In fact, he was now visibly angry.

"I will have to put this in your chart," he said. "You must sign some paperwork stating that you have been informed of all options and are refusing treatment."

"But I don't have anything that needs treatment."

He narrowed his eyes. "As I said, if you have this once,

you'll have it again."

I smiled. "Thanks for believing in me. I will never need this again."

I signed the paperwork and left his office, feeling like I'd just won the biggest battle in my life.

*"We do not see things as they are, we see them as we are."*

*-Anais Nim*

# CHAPTER 37

# Intuition

Awakening takes many forms. It's an ongoing experience, not a singular event. Opportunities to awaken happen more often if we can see them and are ready for them. If we aren't, we continue to experience the same lessons until we do awaken–or until life just ends, like it did for my dad.

I refused to let those doctors instill fear in me. To me, they were powerless, and I was in charge–which is as it should be. It was happening in my body, not theirs.

I'm not against doctors. I know many, and admire them greatly. Doctors are needed, and have their place in the treatment of physical trauma. What I'm against is the lack of humanity in the system, and how it treats symptoms, not root causes. Western medicine considers the body, but it still does not consider the mind, as if they are separate from one another. It often bypasses our family situation, lifestyle, the amount of stress we are exposed to, the childhood we had, and all the experiences and struggles that come with it.

The experience with the mammogram taught me to make conscious, empowered decisions for myself and my own life—not based on empty fiction or what others expect from me. This makes some people around me uneasy, like it did with several of the medical professionals I dealt with during this time. Often, what I want doesn't fit with others' expectations of me, and that's completely normal. Actually, it shows me I'm on the right, aligned path, following my own dream life, not someone else's prescribed version.

When I followed my desire to start a business, this made a lot of people around me uncomfortable, because my choice challenged their belief that security and status equal success.

When someone pushes back or seems genuinely bothered by my choices, I've learned to see it not as a warning sign, but a powerful confirmation. Their discomfort is often about the painful compromises they've told themselves are just "being realistic" or "mature." My clarity can be an unflinching mirror, and sometimes that's deeply threatening to people who are still anxiously negotiating with themselves.

Connecting with my intuition during this time has

only encouraged it to get stronger. This is an active, intentional practice that I choose over and over. I take time to pay attention and listen carefully to my body, noticing any physical sensations before they turn into something bigger and more overwhelming, just like with my dad. The effects appear in all kinds of ways. I'll be thinking of a friend, and suddenly they'll call me. I'll hear a song in the morning, and later in the day, I'll find myself in a situation where that song's lyrics are like a message I needed to hear. I'll shake someone's hand and know their emotional state, or take a different route only to find out I avoided a huge accident.

This unshakeable trust—trust in my intuition; trust that I can gracefully handle whatever unexpected consequences come; trust in the continuous, honest feedback between my deliberate actions and my expanding awareness—isn't recklessness. It's the complete opposite. It's being so present, so finely tuned in, that I can move with genuine confidence and natural ease. I learn through direct, raw experience instead of waiting around endlessly for guaranteed outcomes that never actually come. Sometimes, I just notice and fully enjoy the feeling of being relaxed. I try to notice my racing, wandering thoughts without automatically reacting to everything.

I have learned to live a full, vibrant life without regrets. Nasko and I don't leave any space for "could've, should've, would've." We make our own clear, confident decisions in the present moment, without waiting for external approval or permission. I refuse to alter myself in order to fit in and be accepted, which people have called "selfish", especially when my/our boundaries clash with their expectations of us. We choose to focus on our kids and skiing, disappearing into the mountains for the winter season, which disturbs the social norm to be available; to be part of the pack. People are not used to this. They often prefer it for others to lose themselves in order to fit in. We still make the effort to join larger events when it's humanly possible, but we choose to prioritize ourselves.

And Bella and I are learning, together, to to allow others to step in and give us a hand when we need it.

This is what it means to be truly, vibrantly alive: present, fully embodied, self-directed, and accountable only to the deep, unwavering truth we discover within ourselves. I wouldn't trade this electric aliveness for hollow comfort or empty approval ever again. Which is why I'm so grateful for this whole mammogram experience.

I don't know what would have happened during this time if I hadn't just gone through RTT training. Life slapped me hard, but also, I had come to understand that I held life in my hands. It was all up to me, not anyone else. I knew what I was capable of. I had everything I needed for healing available to me.

And so do you.

*"What happened to you as a child is not your fault.
It happens to you, not with you.
But it is your responsibility to fix it. "*

*- Will Smith*

# CHAPTER 38

# Beliefs

A few final reflections on my RTT journey (so far)

Remember the iceberg cabbage? AKA my first attempt at cooking?

I could have decided that day that cooking was not for me. Luckily, I (subconsciously) chose to be inspired and curious. This is another example of the power of the stories we tell ourselves.

My spice cabinet is now my pride and joy: a fragrant, multicolored library from around the world. I'm always hunting for new spices to experiment with. When I travel, markets are my museums. There's something therapeutic about transforming raw ingredients into a nourishing meal. Maybe that's why I love both cooking and therapy—they're both about transformation, patience, and believing in possibilities that others might not yet see.

***

I have a sign in my kitchen window that says "No Bad Days". It's positioned where I can see it every morning while I make coffee, where my kids can see it while they eat breakfast, and where anyone who enters our home can't miss it. And it works, not by magic, but through gentle, persistent repetition. It shifts our mindset without us paying conscious attention to it. It quietly reminds us: we have a choice. When frustration arises or disappointment hits, the sign is there, redirecting us back to what we've decided: no bad days, just days with inevitable hard moments that we'll get through together.

We began to practice gratitude together at family dinners, where we share at least one thing that we're grateful for from the day. I see how doing this builds relationships, appreciation, and positive emotions, and how it helps us deal with adversity. And honestly, it just feels good.

Of course it's harder on some days than others, but it makes us pay attention to the small moments we might otherwise let pass without noticing. It helps us move the focus away from what we don't have, and it's helped me, personally, be grateful for the generational cycles that limited me in the past, because they've taught me so much, and have helped me empower my kids to continue to upgrade their own, positive habits.

I've learned that happiness is not about denying reality or pretending challenges don't exist. It's about deciding how you'll meet whatever the day brings. Because even when things go wrong, even when life throws curveballs, we get to decide if we let that define an entire day or if we can find something good to hold onto.

***

I recently heard an analogy: when people are comfortable in their cage and you put the key in front of them, some still won't reach for it. For me, one of those cages was my fear of water.

I had been afraid of water for as long as I can remember. No one in my family could recall a specific event that might have instilled this in me. Nasko and the kids enjoyed swimming, and when we traveled, Nasko and Danny would dive in open water while I struggled at the pool, at the lake, and in the ocean, where I always felt the need to feel ground under my feet. The kids and Nasko would stay submerged all day while I sat in the sun and read books. I wanted to share their joy of water, but my fear was stronger.

When I began doing RTT, I took on this fear. My mind brought me back to middle school, where we had weekly swimming classes. One week, I had convinced my teacher that I couldn't go into the water because I was afraid. He was understanding, and let me sit on the bench at the side of the pool. That day, I felt like I was at the center of all the attention. After class, while all my classmates were wet with messy hair, I was untouched. I felt special. Important. Different, in a good way. And it stuck: after that day, I never participated in a swimming class again.

My mind had adopted the lie, turned it into a belief, and prevented me from learning how to swim. With RTT, I understood that this fear was not true. On our next holiday, I tested it by floating in the pool with a noodle. I felt reborn! That same day, I went into the ocean. Nasko and the kids couldn't believe what they were seeing.

Three days after that, I watched Nasko and Daniel go diving in front of our hotel. I thought, "Since they already have the equipment... why don't I just try?" I put on the gear in the pool, and dipped beneath the surface. It was so quiet, like being in another world. It was a peace I had never experienced.

Nasko asked, teasingly, if I wanted to join the dive they had scheduled for the next day. He even texted the guy who worked at the dive shop, who said they could accommodate me. You don't actually have to be able to swim in order to dive, you just have to stay in control, so you don't breathe too fast and ascend too quickly.

So I went with them.

Since Nasko and Danny were certified, they went much deeper. But Bella, the instructor and I still dove down to thirty feet. I got to explore this beautiful underwater world, which moved at its own pace—with so much grace, and such a lack of urgency. It was a sense of freedom I'd never felt before. I felt happiness in every cell of my body.

I had the key. But I had to find it on my own.

This, and many experiences as a therapist, and in life, taught me that I can't change anyone who doesn't see problems in their own actions. If I think this person has opportunities for a better life—for example, to learn to swim—that's my opinion, or my expectation. That expectation can be hurtful or unrealistic to that person, depending on where they are on their journey. Their opinion of what a better life is might be very different from mine. I've learned that people have different value systems, and for some, awakening is not their highest priority. I can't convince anyone to make a shift before they are ready. And I shouldn't have to, although this is often a painful fact to sit with.

Now, I focus on what is good for me, and I let go of expectations from others. My practice has taught me how to read people and to meet them where they are. Sometimes, when I see that a client isn't ready for change with me, I refer them to a colleague.

We are like fruits. A green strawberry isn't going to be sweet. You have to give it time to ripen and be ready. That's why my practice is so customized. I've learned to give people space to move at their own pace. Even if I believe they can move faster, that's not up to me.

***

Being away from my parents kept me out of their everyday lives, and there were many details they didn't share with me because I was "far away". Their belief was: what difference would it make if I knew? Why bother me? My mom even had open-heart surgery without telling me. "I didn't want to worry you," she told me, later. I'm not mad about this, but I see how it's a generational pattern.

Often, when a child asks a parent, "Will I die?", the answer is, "Yes, but not for a very long time. Don't worry about it." We decide that kids are too young to understand death, and teach them to use avoidance to cope with it very early on in life, or to store grief in their bodies, which actually raises their anxiety, even if they don't know it. Later, that anxiety resurfaces into full-blown fear—the kind of fear that, as adults, we often don't know how to deal with.

If an adult is willing to explain death and grieving to a child at their level, the child will understand.

When my dad passed away, even though I hadn't yet started the RTT process, I didn't hide my feelings or my tears. I allowed my kids to see me as I was going through all the stages of grief. When I did begin RTT six months later, I leaned in even more. I wanted to normalize the ups and downs of grieving for them, and for it not to be a stigma. Grieving means we cry one moment and laugh the next. That's how it is.

My kids were curious what happens when someone dies. They had seen a cemetery, and knew that the body went there. But they wanted to know, "What happens to the soul? Does it fly away? If it flies away, where does it go?"

Although these are abstract questions and there are many different beliefs about it, we read about it and decided what it meant to us: "The soul goes to the sky/the universe where it gets reconnected with other souls." This is an open-ended answer that may change and evolve over the years as we gain knowledge, but at least it didn't leave them hanging with the questions. I also learned how important it is to have an organized folder or notebook with all the important details (a will or a trust) to ensure your wishes are respected and honored, to minimize legal complications, and relieve family members of significant administrative burdens.

Being open about death and grieving is part of building character, resilience, and, most importantly, family trust. Experiencing a family death was a critical time to address all the questions they had, especially as it was the first time they were going through the process.

My family's generational beliefs about death and grief stop with me. For us, it's a normal part of the life cycle. I believe that losing a loved one leaves a trail of strong feelings, no matter whether we're an adult or a child. And people experience grief for not only losing a loved one but also for lost experiences, lost self-image, loss of time, and lost objects. In my practice now, I often see people's grief over losing their self-image. It's so hard for many people to accept change, so instead, fear preoccupies their minds and grief preoccupies their hearts. When I moved to the US, I believe I went through a form of that grief–for the old me, for the separation from my parents and friends, and from my country in general. But I wasn't aware of it, and no one ever talked about it, so my generational resilience kicked in and I buried that part of myself, unknowingly–and necessarily, so I could move on. I often see clients grieving for an old version of themselves, and often stuck living from the point of view of that old version, unable to move forward in life.

Grief is a cocktail of many different feelings like sadness, anger, longing, loneliness, guilt, resentment, and regret, but definitely not limited to only those. A cognitive approach is a constructive way of facing those feelings, and in my practice, Rapid Transformational Therapy helps get to the root of the fear and overcome it.

***

Recently, it hit me that Bella, now a teenager, had heard snippets of the Down syndrome story as she was growing up. But the story, I realized, had never been told to her entirely or with the care it deserved. Since I've learned that stories have the power to shape us; to plant seeds that can blossom into beliefs we carry for life, I didn't want Bella to hear only bits and pieces that might later leave her feeling uncertain or burdened by something she never fully understood. I wanted her to feel the depth of our love, the obstacles we faced, and the lengths we went to ensure she arrived healthy and safe.

So one evening, as we settled into the quiet comfort of our home, I told her that story completely, as I shared it with you.

We sat close together, Bella's familiar presence a reminder of all we had been through. I took a deep breath and recounted each step, each fear, and every decision we made with her well-being in mind. As I spoke, I watched her expressions, seeing glimpses of the little girl who once clung to my hand mixed with the understanding of a young woman who knew me well. I told her about the challenges, the doubts, and the unshakeable hope we clung to, all for her.

Bella leaned in at some points in the story, her face serious, absorbing each word. At others, she just hugged me, sensing how much this story meant to us both. We actually exchanged countless hugs throughout the story, an unspoken understanding filling the space between words. I could feel her processing everything, understanding for the first time how deeply we had loved her even before she was born and how much that love had shaped her beginning

"You really wanted me," she said. "You fought for me.

I'm sorry you had to go through that, but I'm happy I'm here."

"Don't be sorry," I said. "I'm sure it happened for a reason. We learned lessons. We learned that we had to stick to our boundaries, and to prioritize our own beliefs first. We learned to listen to our gut."

"How do you listen to your gut?"

"Have you ever been in a situation where your body or gut is telling you what to do? A feeling that you know what the right thing is?"

"Yes. Is that a gut feeling?"

"Yes. And we all have it. The more you use it, the more it appears."

Bella took a deep breath. "Thanks for having me. What would have happened if I'd been a boy?"

"I really wanted a girl and did everything I could to make that happen," I said.

"But if I were a boy, would you have kept trying to have a girl?"

"Yes."

"Mom," Bella said, exhaling. "You have to include this story in your book. I'm really happy that I'm here and that you want me so much. I knew the story, but I didn't know what you went through and how much you wanted me."

And with that, she wrapped her arms around me, and the story, once scattered in fragments, was now something whole, something she could carry forward in her own way.

That evening left us both changed, connected by a reminder of love, resilience, and the strength we drew from each other long before we had met her. In her final hug, I felt a sense of peace, knowing the story now rested in her heart as it was meant to.

Every story is unique, yet when it comes to kids, simplicity speaks volumes. For Bella, understanding how deeply she was wanted has meant everything. It fills her with a sense of belonging; an awareness that she is cherished beyond words. Knowing she is loved, that she was hoped for and celebrated before she even arrived, gives her strength and confidence. This simple but profound story is a gift that I hope stays with her for a lifetime.

***

In his book *The Anatomy of Hope*, Jerome Groopman, MD, writes, "Researchers are learning that a change in mindset has the power to alter neurochemistry. Belief and expectations–the key elements of hope–can block pain by releasing the brain's endorphins and enkephalins, mimicking the effect of morphine."

In order to be in charge of our beliefs and thoughts, we have to first be aware of them. Many live on autopilot in today's buzzy world, unaware of their thoughts, beliefs, and even that their bodies are in pain... never mind that that pain is so often caused by beliefs.

Beliefs are the master commanders of our behavior and its results. Beliefs control our bodies and how we respond to crises, criticism, and opportunities. They tell us what to notice, what to focus on, what it means, and what to do about it. The fact that our beliefs shape our physical, emotional, intellectual, and cultural reality is undeniable. Beliefs create behaviours, and the cumulation of those behaviours adds up to our entire life. In other words, our beliefs determine our destiny.

So: we have a thought, then a feeling arises from that thought, then a behavior arises from that feeling, and then we see the result of that behavior.

Or we have a belief, then a thought that arises from that belief, then a feeling, then a behavior, then a result. Either way, our beliefs will heal us or they will harm us. They either support our aspirations or thwart them. Beliefs become the source of our limitations or of our liberation. It doesn't matter what's true, it matters what we believe. Because whatever you believe, you will strive to achieve.

*"Be happy with what you have,
while working for what you want."*

*- Helen Keller*

# CHAPTER 39

# Forgiveness

In Bulgaria, every year, we have a day called Sirni Zagovezni. It's a day that's dedicated to asking for and giving forgiveness.

As kids, my brothers and I would start in the morning, by asking our parents. Then we'd head to our great-grandparents' house, where we asked everyone else in the family as they arrived: our aunties and uncles, our grandparents, and finally, our great-grandparents.

"May you be forgiven," they would say, or, "May God forgive you."

Since we don't eat meat on Sirni Zagovezni, and it's the last day before Lent to eat anything with animal products, we'd share a meal of boiled eggs, cheese, boiled wheat, dried fruits, and roasted pumpkin. After dinner, my great-grandfather would do the hamkane, a tradition where the oldest man in the house hangs white halva (a sticky candy made from a local herb, sugar syrup, and nuts) on a red thread. He would spin it in a circle, and each member of the family, but mainly the kids, tried to catch the halva with their mouths. I love this day, and I know my father loved it, too. He loved every occasion when we gathered as much of the family as possible in the same place.

I had spent so much time trying to understand my dad, and trying to unravel what was behind all the habits and ideas he held onto so tightly. But after many of my questions had been answered, one still lingered.

Why hadn't I gone to see him in Bulgaria when he was nearing the end of his life? And why didn't I go to his funeral?

There were obvious reasons, of course. COVID-19 restrictions. Having a family to take care of (although after all the learning I've done, I know now that they would have been fine without me). But these were excuses, not truths. The borders hadn't shut down by the time my father passed away. If I'd really wanted to go, nothing would have stopped me. So, what held me back?

My father had taught me to never give up. No matter what happens, you get up, dust yourself off, and keep going. But in my eyes, in the most critical fight of his life, he'd surrendered. And although it took me a long time to see, I eventually understood what I actually felt towards him.

It was anger.

I was furious that he had, as I saw it, given up on life and left me behind. I was enraged that he, who had instilled so much resilience in me, had abandoned that resilience when it mattered most. That he'd done the exact opposite of what he'd spent a lifetime teaching me to do.

Of course this was all subconscious—his actions, and my thoughts about them. I didn't see that I'd felt betrayed by him. I'd simply absorbed the hurt, carrying it with me like a shadow, until it finally came out into the light.

I've come to learn that for many women, our relationship with our father falls into one of two categories: unwavering hero, or source of heartbreak. This relationship colors the way we view the world, and our place in it. For those of us with hero fathers, our bond with them can be a fortress of love and support. But a fortress can also be a barrier. A future partner might find themselves playing second fiddle, with their every gesture and intention overshadowed by a larger-than-life father figure. Or we might, as I did, adopt the "I can do everything myself" attitude, which usually leads to burnout, and can be disempowering for a partner, and for our kids. A woman with a hero dad might even be hesitant to allow another man to take up space in her heart. After all, how could anyone compare to the man who defined her sense of safety and who holds all her admiration?

There's another side to that coin, too: the deep, aching

disappointment that can arise when our hero falls from grace. This heartbreak can be more painful than any flesh wound, and can feel as significant as the loss of a loved one, or the trauma of abuse. But the scars it leaves behind often go unnoticed, leaving only a ghostly sense of betrayal.

I'd felt betrayed because of my expectations of my father as my hero. That's why I hadn't gone to see him before he passed, or gone to his funeral. This betrayal was what I had such a hard time swallowing. It's what was really hurting me.

By the time I figured this out, I'd done so much RTT, had learned so much, had changed so much, and had accepted so much that I hadn't understood before. So as soon as I recognized that I'd been carrying this anger, I also understood that my father simply hadn't known how to fight. He'd done the best he could. He most likely had no idea that he wasn't just fighting an illness, but childhood trauma. It was not in his control, and what I had done—and hadn't done—wasn't in mine.

I've learned that forgiveness is not for the other person. We do it for ourselves. As I began to understand that abuse can pass from one generation to the next without a person realizing it, I was able to let go of my dad's story, and of my anger about how he let me down. I was also able to let go of the story that my parents were emotionally unavailable, even though I wished they had been more present for me. I no longer wanted these stories to define me.

And I forgave myself. For the mistakes I made. For the opportunities I missed. For the times I fell short.

I know so much more about my father now. I can put myself in his shoes, and feel how difficult life must have felt for him. And I know I'm blessed. My parents managed to keep much of their childhood adversity to themselves, and not repeat it on us. But many parents do treat their children as they themselves were treated, because they had no healthy role models and were never able to heal or correct their own behaviour.

It is commonly said that grief lessens with time. I don't believe this is true. Grief stays the same, but life starts to grow around it. We process the stages of grief in our own time. My dad did his best at being resilient and stopping some of his generational cycles, and he did it in the only way he knew how. I can learn, from his approach, what not to do. It's my turn to be a generational cycle breaker—with awareness, curiosity, and compassion. And with the hope that I will be a better example for my kids and future generations.

I had held onto my father as if he were a lifesaver in a stormy sea.

Now, finally, I could let him go.

*"Family –
a little bit of crazy,
a little bit of loud,
and a whole lot of love."*

*- Unknown*

# CHAPTER 40

# **Memories**

In 2019, Nasko and I bought a house in Plovdiv, very close to where my family's old mushroom farm used to be. We visit as often as we can. Every time we do, my nieces, nephews, brothers, and sister-in-law have dinner at our house almost every night. They have their own homes, of course—just down the road. But when Nasko, I, and the kids are in Bulgaria, our place becomes a centrifugal force, just like my great-grandparents' place was during Sirni Zagovezni. Dad was obsessed with togetherness. When we were growing up, he always wanted to have as many friends over as he could fit. That's a generational pattern I love repeating.

I have so many memories of playing under the walnut tree at my great-grandparents' house, and eating its nuts. In honor of them, I had a table made out of walnut wood for our home in Plovdiv. It's over 16 feet long, which means that my brothers, my sisters-in-law, their kids, Nasko, me, and our kids–plus a few guests–can all sit comfortably at it.

Dad also used to say, "You know you had enough food when you have leftovers." (Of course, this points to another pattern of the safety of having food... from a time where we weren't sure if we would eat the next day... but you know that by now. And we all, as an extended family, are working on overcoming that pattern.)

Anyway, these prized gatherings around that table are my parents' legacy, and especially my father's. Now, we're passing a new, hopefully improved version down to our kids. Whether we're in Plovdiv or in Seattle, eating dinner together is a time to have open conversations, where everyone is included. It's a time where we share a pause, strengthen our bonds, and reaffirm our love and care for one another. The dinner table is a sanctuary; a place to lay down our burdens. It's a reminder that no matter what the day brings, we're in it together.

***

Two years after my father died, after one of those huge family dinners, we all gathered–me and my brothers and our spouses and all of our kids–around the TV.

My mom had found a box full of rolls of film he had recorded with his camera and his video camera. When we'd returned to Plovdiv, Nasko and I found a service and had them all digitized.

Now, together, we watched the moments in time my father had meticulously recorded but had never seen.

Instantly, we all started shouting over each other: first my brothers and I, then the kids.

"That was Grandpa being Santa Claus!"

"I knew first!"

"No, *I* knew first!"

"But you didn't say anything!"

"I didn't want to spoil the fun for you all! Plus, we were getting presents."

There was my mom, pregnant with the twins. There was my dad, his face aglow, holding two babies. Graduations, parties, the yarn manufacturing, the Herbalife gatherings. There were photos of us from school with friends, which led to more shouted stories about what had happened to each of them. Birthdays... early family vacations during communism... dressing up the family dog in our clothes. The first time Nasko returned to Bulgaria.

"Is that *you*, Mom?"

"Look at your hair!"

"Your mom was in a class with just boys, and let me tell you, she was the queen."

There were even photos of my parents' wedding, in color, which sent us into new levels of hysteria.

"Look at mom's hat!"

"Look how HOT they were!"

My brothers and I all had different stories and memories about the exact same photos. Each one had us all jumping up and down and yelling—especially as most of the videos were silent, so we added our own dialogue of what our parents would have said. The kids were beside themselves.

It felt like magic.

It felt, in a way, in fact, like messages that were sent forward in time... from my grandparents and my parents... from my younger self to me right now, sitting here, in our home in Plovdiv, with my own kids, watching.

*We are a family,* they were telling us.

*We always have come together as a family, and we always will.*

*Yes, we carry many stories... but not all of them are heavy. Many hold light. And laughter, and goodness, and joy. Not all generational cycles need healing. Some... need celebrating.*

*And from the rest... we will heal.*

Because in those photos and in those videos, I could see the truth.

No matter what, we had been cared for, and totally, completely loved.

# About the Author

Diana was born and raised in Bulgaria and has called Seattle home for over twenty years. She is a wife, a mom, and a hypnotherapist whose practice is devoted to helping others break free from generational cycles that quietly shape our lives.

This book was born from her own awakening. As Diana's process became more conscious, something shifted within her — a realization that the only thing standing between her and her dream to write a book was her own beliefs and the discouraging stories running through her mind. She refused to let those limiting beliefs define her. She chose to challenge them, to rewrite the narrative of her own potential, and in doing so, discovered the work she was meant to share with the world.

Outside of her practice, Diana recharges through creativity and nature. She loves art in all its forms and finds deep joy in making things with her own hands. Nature trips bring the ultimate clarity to the mind. Travel is another of her great loves — exploring new countries, meeting people from different cultures, learning how they live, think, and move through the world. She is endlessly curious about food, often challenging herself to recreate dishes she's tasted abroad. Her curiosity is the force that keeps her moving forward, always toward new places, new people, and new understanding.

Generational Resilience is her first book, and she would love to hear your story.

You can connect with Diana:
Book: www.generationalresilience.com

Practice: www.revealedmind.com,

Instagram & YouTube: @revealedmind

Free 30-minute consultations available through her website.

# Acknowledgments

I give thanks to all generations that are the reason for me to be here.

To my grandmother Dima, for the unconditional love and always being willing to be there for me.

To my mother, Blaga, and my late father, Nasko. For giving me life and providing the calm and loving environment in which I grew up. Even though I lost my dad before I got to know him, I know that he loved me, and he was always there for me. Every moment of my childhood shaped me to be who I am today. It gave me a lot of awareness and the strength to overcome the struggles presented to me.

To my husband's mother, Petia, and his father, Mitko, who gave him life. For all the times they challenged me and fired me to be the best version of myself.

I am profoundly grateful for my brothers Ivan and Hristo, with whom I grew up close, and we are still very close, and their wives, Boyana and Yordanka, for their unwavering support. Their unconditional love has been a source of strength and encouragement, fostering a deep connection and shared resilience within our family bonds.

To my brother-in-law, Hristo, who captured my heart as a sweet little boy.

I am grateful for the many family members, friends, teachers, colleagues, and strangers whom I haven't mentioned by name but who have left an incredible mark on my life. I am grateful for how you shaped me - whether for a moment or much longer, your presence has mattered.

I am grateful to all of you who, in one way or another, encouraged me to write this book. For those of you who were next to me in the process, and those who never stopped believing I would publish it. For all of you eagerly waiting to read it, you all matter to me.

I am grateful to Janice Finch, who gave me constructive feedback on my first piece of writing; she encouraged me when doubts clouded my vision. I learned a lot.

I am grateful to my neighbor Moniece Rae Charlton and her connections for helping me find a great editor.

I am grateful to my editor, Natalie Karneef, who clicked with me and jumped into this huge project, willing to be my editor, mentor, and coach.

I am grateful to my chiropractor Dana McCracken for

keeping me align try this journey - yes emotions and feelings have the power to move bones.

Although this book is dedicated to my husband and kids, I want to acknowledge them again. They stood by me and allowed me to share our stories. This book has been a labor of love and honesty. I thought I understood what that saying meant until I had to labor in the love of birthing this book. Sometimes stories were too heavy, and I had to stop and allow myself to process them and then continue to write. There were moments when I was uncomfortable being so vulnerable; my family stood by me. By writing this book, they allowed me the space to get it all out with clarity and more to tell. I went to places and moments I thought I had left behind, and they stood by me. Having them with me made me brave on the journey and opened my eyes.

And thank YOU for joining me on this journey and for giving me the gift of your time. I don't take this life for granted, and I am grateful that you have chosen to take time from your life to learn about mine. I hope that my stories will give you permission to be the perfectly imperfect parent and to be you. Just like the Japanese technique Kintsugi, where they pick up the broken pieces of pottery and weld them back together with gold, I hope these stories have inspired you to pick up the broken pieces of your life and put them together in a more beautiful way. Today, I can look back on my life and see the beautiful experiences beyond what was broken.

# Notes

P.8 - Quote: "You are given this life, because you are strong enough to live it."- Robin Sharma, book "The Monk Who Sold His Ferrari"

P.14 - Quote: "Who looks outside - dreams; who looks inside - awakes."- Carl Jung, book "Letters Volume I"

P.22 - Quote: "Adolescents need freedom to choose, but not so much that they cannot, in fact, make a choice." - Erik Erikson, book "Identity: Youth and Crisis"

P.28 Quote: "If I ever tell you about my past, it's never because I want you to feel sorry for me, but so you can understand why I am who I am."- Unknown

P.34 Quote: "Many will choose stability of slavery over uncertainty of freedom" - Marcus Aurelius

P.42 Quote: "Love felt by the parent does not automatically translate in to love experienced by the child"- Dr. Gabor Maté, book "Scattered Minds: The Origins and Healing of Attention Deficit Disorder"

P.50 Quote: "If we are not prepared to think for ourselves, and make the effort to learn how to do this well, we will always be in danger of becoming slaves to the ideas and values of others due to our own ignorance."- William Hughes, book "Critical Thinking: An Introduction to the Basic Skills"

P.56 Quote: "Whiners find ways to complain while winners find ways to succeed" - Joe Polish,his publication, The Little Book of Ass Kickers.

P.62 Quote: "Every time I thought I was being rejected from

something good, I was actually being re-directed to something better." - Dr. Steve Maraboli, book Unapologetically You: Reflections on Life and the Human Experience

P. 63 Multi-level marketing (MLM), also called network marketing or pyramid selling, is a controversial and sometimes illegal marketing strategy for the sale of products or services in which the revenue of the MLM company is derived from a non-salaried workforce selling the company's products or services, while the earnings of the participants are derived from a pyramid-shaped or binary compensation commission system. Source by https://www.wikipedia.org/

P.63. Herbalife Nutrition Ltd., also called Herbalife International, Inc. (with a U.S. subsidiary called Herbalife International of America) or simply Herbalife, is an American multinational multi-level marketing (MLM) corporation that develops and sells dietary supplements. The company has been alleged to have fraudulently operated a pyramid scheme; under an SEC agreement in 2016 the compensation and other benefits were restructured to include tying distributor rewards to verifiable sales. Some products sold by Herbalife have caused acute hepatitis.[5] The business is incorporated in the Cayman Islands, a tax haven, with its corporate headquarters located in Los Angeles, California. - source by https://www.wikipedia.org/

P.64 "...in 2023, fewer than 1% of active participants earned income in the six-figure range the FTC alleges Wellington promised." see full article by Federal Trade Commissioner here

P.70 Quote: "And ever has it been known that love knows not its own depth until the hour of separation."- Khalil Gibran, book The Prophet

P.76 Quote: "Strong women aren't simply born. They are made

by the storm they walk through." -Unknown

P.82 Quote: "Not being able to speak is not the same as not having anything to say."- Rosemary Crossley, book "Speechless: Facilitating Communication for People Without Voices"

P.83. - According to the European Parliament, during the 1990s, over 500,000 people left Bulgaria

P.86 Quote: "Only those who will risk going too far, can possibly find out how far one can go."- T.S. Eliot, book "The Idea of a Christian Society"

P.90 Quote: "We have to get use to the idea – at the most important crossroads in our life there are no signs."- Eenest Hemingway

P.96 Quote: "When someone tells you 'That's impossible', remember that they're talking about their own possibilities, not your limitations. - Unknown

P. 104 Quote: "To be away from home and yet find oneself everywhere at home; to see the world,to be at the center of the world, and yet remain hidden from the world." - Charles Baudelaire, his essay "The Painter of Modern Life"

P.106 VHS - VHS (Video Home System) is a discontinued standard for consumer-level analog video recording on tape cassettes, introduced in 1976 by JVC. It was the dominant home video format throughout the tape media period of the 1980s and 1990s. Source by https://en.wikipedia.org/wiki/VHS

P.108 ESL stands for English as a Second Language, referring to programs and instruction for non-native speakers learning English, focusing on reading, writing, listening, and speaking skills in English-speaking environments. - source by https://www.wikipedia.org/

P.110 Quote: "Growth is uncomfortable; you have to embrace the discomfort if you want to expand" – Jonathan Majors

P.112 "Growth is uncomfortable; you have to embrace the discomfort if you want to expand"– Jonathan Majors

P.116 Quote: "Real intimacy isn't built in the bedrooms but in conversations where your raw thoughts, fears, and truths are met with love, patience, and a desire to understand."

- Steve De'lano Garcia, book "Edge of the Abyss."

P.122 Quote: "We have all known the long loneliness and we have learned that the only solution is love and that love comes with community,"- Dorothy Day, book "The Long Loneliness"

P. 128 Quote: "Love doesn't make the world go 'round. Love is what makes the ride worthwhile."- Franklin P. Jones

P.132 Quote: "Having a baby is a life-changer. It gives you a whole other perspective on why you wake up every day." - Taylor Hanson

P.138 Quote: "Parenting is the easiest thing in the world to have an opinion about and the hardest thing in the world to do"- Matt Walsh, his article titled "An Uncensored True Tale of Parenting"

P.144 Quote: "If parenthood came with GPS, it would mostly just say,… 'recalculating.'"

- Simon Holland

P. 150 Quote: "Spending time with children is more important than spending money on children." - Anthony Douglas Williams, book "Inside the Divine Pattern"

P.156 Quote: "The sun always shines above the clouds"- Paul Davis

P. 168 Quote: "When you lost your voice, you lost the ability to make sense of yourself" — Yōko Ogawa, book " The Memory Police '

P.172 Quote: "Doing your best is more important than being the best" - Zig Ziglar

P.173 Kanzashi (簪)  are hair ornaments used in traditional Japanese hairstyles. The term kanzashi refers to a wide variety of accessories, including long, rigid hairpins, barrettes, fabric flowers and fabric hair ties.

In the English-speaking world, the term kanzashi is typically used to refer to hair ornaments made from layers of folded cloth used to form flowers (tsumami kanzashi), or the technique of folding used to make the flowers.

P.178 Quote: " When you travel with children you are giving something that can never be taken away...experience exposure and a way of life."-Pamela Chandle

P. 186 Quote: "The best education you will ever get is traveling. Nothing teaches you more than exploring the world and accumulating experiences." - Mark Paterson

P.190 Quote: "So, our job as parents is not to make a particular kind of child. Instead, our job is to provide a protected space of love, safety, and stability in which children of many unpredictable kinds can flourish."- Alison Gopnik, book "The Gardener and the Carpenter."

P. 196 Quote: "The most dangerous phrase in language is: "We've always done it this way" - Grace Hopper

P.204 Quote: "Never be a prisoner of your past. It was just a lesson, not a life sentence."- unknown

P. 216 Quote: "It is not what you are that holds you back. It is what you think you are not. You are always one decision away from a totally different life." - Mel Robbins, book "The 5 Second Rule."

P. 222 Quote: "Healthy habits are learned in the same way as unhealthy ones - try practice." - Wayne Dyer, book "Pulling Your Own Strings "

P. 226 Quote: "The secret of change is to focus all of your energy not on fighting the old, but on building the new."- Dan Millman , book "Way of the Peaceful Warrior"

P.230 <u>Kintsugi</u> "golden joinery", also known as "golden repair", is the Japanese art of repairing broken pottery by mending the areas of breakage with urushi lacquer dusted or mixed with powdered gold, silver, or platinum. The method is similar to the maki-e technique. As a philosophy, it treats breakage and repair as part of the history of an object, rather than something to disguise.

P. 232 Quote: "Death is the enemy of the dead; grief is the enemy of the living." - William Shakespeare

P. 238 Quote: "History is not destiny, our past could be understood, but it doesn't dictate our present and our future. We don't have to run from our past nor we have to be insulted by it." -Tina Bryson, book "The Power of Showing Up"

P.241 Root cause work is not the same as regression therapy, although they are often confused. Regression therapy deliberately guides someone back into past scenes, memories or imagined timelines to re-experience them emotionally. The aim is catharsis, release or narrative change. Root cause work is an outcome-driven investigation, using memory, sensation and belief to locate the first moment a pattern was formed, whether or not it looks dramatic or story-like. You cannot find a root cause without some form of regression process, but the regression is only the tool, not the therapy - Source by RTT school

p. 246. Quote: "Enough with the puppet show we play for everyone. It is time to live for ourselves." Srimanju Katragadda

P.248 Quote: "Once you surrender to living in your truth, in your light, and in your love, it shall set you free. When you are ready to be the change in your life, to break down the rules and walls that trap you, to make a new way out of no way, and breakthrough to your freedom, the universe shows up out of nowhere to help you do it." - Zainab Salbi - book "Freedom Is an Inside Job"

p. 252 Quote: "The moment you change your perception; is the moment you rewrite the chemistry of your body."- Dr. Bruce Lipton - book "The Biology of Belief"

P.249 "...The second group had an equal number of sessions with a psychologist who gave emotional support but no hypnotic intervention. The third group received only standard postoperative care.

Nurses examined the surgical wounds over seven postoperative weeks, without knowing to which of the groups patients belonged. They judged that the surgical wounds of the group receiving hypnosis healed faster than those receiving only supportive attention, who in turn healed faster than the group with only standard postoperative care. Statistically, the differences were so large that they would have occurred by chance less than once in a thousand cases. A team of doctors who studied digital photographs of the wounds made judgments in the same direction, although not at a statistically significant level.

"This is still just the beginning of the story," says Ginandes. "The bottom line is that the field of hypnosis is lagging in clinical trials far behind what we know to be true clinically. There's a lot of anecdotal evidence that mind-body healing is a true phenomenon, but the challenge is to prove it in a scientifically acceptable way. "See full article "Hypnosis Heals" by Jerry Shine, Harvard Magazine here

P.249 "...Hypnotic analgesia also prevents pain-related cardiovascular response: therefore, it may stand comparison with pharmacological anesthesia, yielding true protection from stress for the patient. The wealth of data available in the literature provides clear evidence of its meaningful effects on perioperative emotional distress, pain, medication consumption, physiological parameters, duration of surgery and outcome. Hypnosis may be used as follows: 1) as sole anesthetic, in minor surgery and invasive maneuvers and/or selected patients; 2) as adjuvant of pharmacological anesthesia (local anesthesia and/or sedation); 3) as an adjuvant technique in both pre- and postoperative phases in patients submitted to general anesthesia. Hypnosis, unlike any other therapeutic tools, does not call for drugs or equipment and is an attractive technique: it is free of charge, not burdened with proved adverse events and promises to help improving cost/benefits ratio. "See full article "Hypnosis and anesthesia: back to the future" by Enrico Facco, PubMed here

P.262 Quote: "We do not see things as they are, we see them as we are." - Anaïs Nin - book "Seduction of the Minotaur"

P.268 Quote: "What happened to you as a child is not your fault. It happens to you, not with you. But it is your responsibility to fix it. "- Will Smith - he shared in a 2018 video

P.282 Quote: "Be happy with what you have, while working for what you want." - Helen Keller, essays "The Story of My Life"

P. 288 Quote: "Family - A little bit crazy, a little bit loud, and a whole lot of love."

- Unknown

Diana Oskov